Keep walking in
service to others!

Mollie

Praise for *Walking with Justice*

"Not since *Tuesdays with Morrie* have I witnessed such an endearing love affair between a student of life and a masterful teacher. *Walking with Justice* offers a fresh look at the ageless principles of living and loving from the heart."

—Marci Shimoff, *NY Times* bestselling author of *Love for No Reason*

"*Walking with Justice* is not just a book about seeking justice and doing what's right, but also a manifesto that will help you think bigger about who you are and what you offer the world. This book is transformational and its author a loving teacher committed to your future."

—Michael Port, *NY Times* bestselling author of *The Think Big Manifesto*

"Many thanks to Mollie Marti for bringing the story of her mentor and friend, Judge Max Rosenn, to a larger audience. He set a high standard for what it is to be a just and compassionate human being. We can all learn from his sterling example."

—Daniel H. Pink, *NY Times* bestselling author of *DRIVE* and *A Whole New Mind*

"This must-read book at once entertains, educates, and inspires. Upon first reading, *Walking with Justice* already felt like coming home to a timeless classic."

—Dr. Larina Kase, author of *The Confident Leader*

"*Walking with Justice* contains life vitamins to strengthen readers for a lifetime of morality, service to others, and wise decision making. It belongs in every home, school, and place of worship. Mollie Marti has penned a gift to you and all mankind."

—Frank McKinney, bestselling author of *The Tap, Burst This!*, and others

"This book of profound life wisdom, written with the unassuming touch of a Midwest farm girl's insight, will give you a deeper understanding of where you've been, who you are, and the path forward that is your destiny. This tribute to an extraordinary man is a gift to us all."

—Marshall Ulrich, author of *Running on Empty*

"A wonderful, inspiring, empowering invitation to enrich our lives through the love and lessons of our teachers. In the footsteps of her mentor, Dr. Mollie teaches with such compassion and wisdom that you won't realize you're learning . . . until you suddenly realize that this book has forever changed how you live."

—Dondi Scumaci, author of *Designed for Success*

"As a teacher, Judge Rosenn was patient, kind, and precise. As a jurist he was fair, compassionate, and principled. As family, he was warm, caring, and devoted. Decades after finishing my clerkship I keep a picture of Judge on my desk. It reminds me of the way people are supposed to live."

—Richard Gelfond, CEO, IMAX Corporation

"For each of the past 30 years, Judge Rosenn has made an appearance for my students—the hero of life lessons as a lawyer, as a community leader, and as a person. His lessons, advice, and warmth live on in his law clerks and in those we mentor. Mollie Marti's special tribute to our hero made me laugh. It made me cry. And it gave me the gift of spending time with my life's greatest mentor. All who worked with Judge saw his justice and compassion at work daily in every contribution, every phone call taken, every letter answered. He lived his life to serve, and those around him grew by his very presence. A presence that lives on through the pages of *Walking with Justice*."

—Richard Matasar, Dean of New York Law School

"I am very pleased that Mollie Marti has written a book about one of the most inspirational people in my life. At the end of my clerkship, Judge Rosenn supported my decision to pass up a job on Wall Street to work for a legal aid project. Over the years, the lessons I learned from him have helped keep my perspective on what is truly important in life—to serve others."

—Paul MacGregor, Rosenn law clerk, 1970-71

"A man of extraordinary compassion and wisdom, Judge insisted that his clerks visit federal prisons to understand what it means on a human level to affirm a conviction. While in his nineties, he mastered and shaped complex laws regulating computer and cell phone technology. As *Walking with Justice* highlights, although Judge had an extraordinary impact on the law, his character is his legacy."

—Quentin Palfrey, Rosenn law clerk, 2002-3

"Judge Rosenn took me under his wing after I graduated law school. In the middle of all his enormous responsibilities, he would call to ask me to dinner or tell me about things he felt would be of interest to me. He loved the law and embraced it as the source of our liberty and our freedom, feeling an enormous obligation, like a soldier in battle, to never stop his pursuit of justice. With his death, we lost a treasure. With *Walking with Justice*, we've gained one."

—Judge Joseph Cosgrove, Wilkes-Barre, Pennsylvania

Walking
with
Justice

Uncommon Lessons *from*
One of Life's Greatest Mentors

Mollie Marti, J.D., Ph.D.

GREENLEAF
BOOK GROUP PRESS

Published by Greenleaf Book Group Press
Austin, Texas
www.gbgpress.com

Distributed by Greenleaf Book Group LLC

For ordering information or special discounts for bulk purchases, please contact Greenleaf Book Group LLC at PO Box 91869, Austin, TX 78709, 512.891.6100.

Design and composition by Greenleaf Book Group LLC
Cover design by Greenleaf Book Group LLC

Publisher's Cataloging-In-Publication Data
(Prepared by The Donohue Group, Inc.)
Marti, Mollie Weighner.
  Walking with justice : uncommon lessons from one of life's greatest mentors / Mollie Marti. — 1st ed.
    p. ; cm.
    ISBN: 978-1-60832-235-0

  1. Rosenn, Max, 1910-2006. 2. Rosenn, Max, 1910-2006—Philosophy. 3. Marti, Mollie Weighner—Friends and associates. 4. Marti, Mollie Weighner—Career in law. 5. Self-actualization. 6. Conduct of life. I. Title.
KF373.R76 M27 2012   2011931384

Part of the Tree Neutral® program, which offsets the number of trees consumed in the production and printing of this book by taking proactive steps, such as planting trees in direct proportion to the number of trees used: www.treeneutral.com

TreeNeutral®

Printed in the United States of America on acid-free paper

12 13 14 15 16   10 9 8 7 6 5 4 3 2 1

First Edition

This book is dedicated to the Rosenn law clerks.

We studied by the side of a master weaver.
His colors run through the tapestries of our lives.
You honor him as you weave your own masterpiece of a well-lived life.

Author's Note

This story spans twenty years. It begins in 1991, the year I had a heart transplant. The surgery was done without scalpel or hospitalization. The physician was not a doctor but a lawyer.

I was fresh out of law school and moved across the country from Iowa to Wilkes-Barre, Pennsylvania, to clerk for Judge Max Rosenn of the United States Court of Appeals for the Third Circuit. I went to learn the law. His lessons transformed my life.

Clerking for Judge gave me admission into a privileged group of young lawyers who served him for the three decades he was on the bench. It was part of our shared destiny to be called to study by the side of a master. I write this story of our teacher with great love and respect for each of you.

All conversations and events are true. They come from Judge, his two sons and their families, my co-clerks, and dear mutual friends. I am eternally grateful to all of you for the role you played in this story and in my life.

Few people get to experience a mentor of the judge's caliber. He was a man whose actions truly reflected what gave the greatest meaning to his life. And the thing Max Rosenn found most meaningful was service to others.

Have you ever had a teacher who taught that it is your service to humanity that defines the quality of your life? If so, count yourself fortunate. If not, I would be honored to share the lessons of one such man with you.

Thank you for joining me on this walk with justice.

Contents

Author's Note	vii
Foreword	xi
A Mentor of Mentors	1
An Eagle's View	7
Wearing Humanity Lightly	15
Breaking Bread—With an Apple	21
Mentorship Dance	31
Hospital Justice	41
The Making of a Lawyer	45
A Man of the People	51
Calm Waters Run Deep	59
Gifts and Presence	65
Faith, Hope, and Love	71
Prayers Big and Small	77
A Matter of Faith	81
Life's Regrets	89

Walking with Justice	95
Humility and Honor	101
The Storyteller	107
A Patriot's Heart	115
Military and Civility	121
Destiny Calls	127
Justice for All	131
A Judge's Judge	137
Quiet Leader	143
In Giving We Receive	149
There Was a Teacher	155
In Service to Destiny	161
The Finale	167
Epilogue: Wherever I Go	169
Acknowledgments	177
Rosenn Law Clerks	183
Ode to a Mentor	185
Bonus Chapters	191
About the Author	193

Foreword

Derived from the eponymous Greek god of Homer's mythology, a "mentor" is defined in *Webster's Dictionary* as "a trusted counselor or guide."

Many of us are lucky to have mentors who come along at times in our lives when we need them most. If we are extremely fortunate, these mentors are wise, kind, generous, caring, and just. One of my most valued mentors fits both the dictionary definition and my personal description of desired mentor traits. Her name is Dr. Mollie Marti.

Both a doctor and a lawyer by training, and a business and success coach by design, Dr. Mollie represents everything one could ask for in a mentor. She is indeed wise, kind, generous, caring, and just. And there is something else special about her: everyone who meets her *loves* her.

I had often wondered just how she got that way. Certainly, to a significant degree, it is the result of a good set of genes: Dr. Mollie came from a family that exemplified goodness. However, another key aspect of it turns out to be . . . *her* mentor. And that is what and who this amazing book is about.

His name was Max Rosenn, and he was a judge. A federal appeals judge, to be exact. However, while this title in itself brings with it much honor and regard, that is just a tiny part of who he was. "Judge," as he was referred to by the many who loved him, was what in Hebrew would be called a *tzadik*: a righteous man.

Reading through the pages of this delightful and wisdom-filled book, you will meet a man who embodied everything we would want a fellow human being—and especially a person of high influence—to be. He was kind to all, regardless of their status. He was compassionate, charitable, and exceedingly humble. He worked tirelessly right up until he passed (at age ninety-six!) to be sure his decisions from the bench represented justice and fairness to all concerned. That he was also brilliant and hugely respected by his peers is important; the love, regard and appreciation they had for him as a person is even more important, and far more telling.

While reading *Walking with Justice*, you might discover—as I did—that you have found another mentor: Judge Rosenn himself. Fortunately for us, his protégé has done such a beautiful job of relating the lessons she learned from Judge that you'll be able to determine your best course of action in any given situation by referring back to the book you hold in your hands. If you have any question regarding how to live a good, productive, and righteous life, the answer lies somewhere in these pages. In fact, I would go so far as to say that Dr. Mollie has written a timeless handbook for being human.

Judge Rosenn, I miss you. I only wish I'd had the honor of meeting you. And Dr. Mollie Marti, thank you, thank you, thank you for sharing your mentor with us!

—*Bob Burg, coauthor of the international bestseller* The Go-Giver

A Mentor of Mentors

As I was walking down the hallway of the Iowa College of Law one afternoon in early 1990, my professor beckoned me into his office. He didn't mince words. "Mollie, I have two things to say to you." He pointed his index finger in the air. "First, you need to apply for a federal clerkship." He added another finger to emphasize his point. "Second, you need to apply for a clerkship with Judge Max Rosenn."

As my advisor for the *Iowa Law Review*, Rick Matasar had seen me through some turbulent waters. I was senior articles editor, in charge of reviewing submissions from faculty members across the country and managing a staff of editors. Rick mentored me through a crash course in handling political pressure.

"I'm not familiar with the clerkship process. Tell me more."

"A federal clerkship is quite a feather in the hat of a lawyer. The application process is competitive, but you've already jumped through the biggest hoops by earning strong grades and a law review position. You may even be able to earn a clerkship with a United States Supreme Court Justice upon completing your appellate court clerkship."

"And what is so special about Judge Rosenn?"

"Clerking for any judge is a chance to learn about law, lawyers, and society. Clerking for Judge Rosenn is a chance to learn about these things from a master. He led me to appreciate what many lawyers and judges fail to see: that every word matters, that loose words can cause harm to real people in the real world, and that a judge owes a fidelity to the law beyond his own agenda."

Rick paused as his mind traveled back in time. "I remember asking him as a young clerk, 'What is the quality of justice?' He responded, 'It is fairness.' He taught me not to seek the truth, but the truth of the case."

Wanting to hear more about this man who strongly shaped my own mentor, I quietly settled into the chair by Rick's desk.

"Judge Rosenn has a clear first rule for judging, lawyering, and living life: when in doubt act humanely. Be fair, use the law to reach just conclusions, and protect those who need the most protection. He stands for decency and is known for it when deciding cases. No cheap shots allowed. No matter how outrageous the views or conduct of the lawyers or other members of the bench, he shows respect to them and they return the favor. Each person he meets receives a kind word, and they return kind words to him."

As I listened to Rick describe how the judge shaped the way he looked at the world and his profession, it struck me how much emphasis he was placing on intangibles and values well beyond the learning of the law.

"Judge showed me the importance of having beliefs and letting them guide me in times of doubt. Remain open-minded, and admit when you're wrong. Be humble yet confident enough to know when to fight for what is right, when to compromise when it does not really hurt, and when to let the other guy win, even though you might prevail after a fight."

A piece of a puzzle fell into place. The man who had deftly guided me through law review politics, teaching me when to yield and when to stand my ground, had in turn been schooled by his mentor. A feeling of anticipation began to form that told me my life was about to take a new course that would greatly impact my future.

"The lessons you learn from Judge Rosenn will carry you through the rest of your legal career. He taught me daily to find fulfillment in the law by helping others before helping myself, by giving back to my communities more than I have received, and by being a public servant while building my own career.

"At their best, clerkships provide young lawyers with role models for the future. Judge Rosenn provides the best of the best." Rick leaned forward. "Mollie, if you clerk for Judge, I expect that your year in Wilkes-Barre will stand out as one of the most memorable of your career."

I left my professor's office with a deep curiosity. Who was this teacher in Pennsylvania who lit a fire within my mentor that burned bright with respect decades after his clerkship? I headed to the law library and fired up Westlaw, a legal database. Rick hadn't mentioned his mentor's political leanings. A classic political hot button would provide the easiest litmus test. I typed "Judge Max Rosenn; abortion."

Several cases came up. I clicked on the first one. The court was reviewing a parental notification statute that required a minor to get written approval of both parents for an abortion. Judge Rosenn addressed the complex privacy rights issues in eloquent language. He acknowledged the sanctity of human life, the evils that accompany the likes of abortion, and the government's strong interest in maintaining family solidarity. Looking at the evidence, he acknowledged the plight of the teenage girl and noted that her father had deserted the family and his where-abouts were unknown. He concluded that the law as written did not help the family situation or the social problems, and he ruled that it was overbroad.

Ahh, so this judge was pro-choice.

I clicked on the next case. The decision addressed picketing in front of an abortion clinic. Again, Judge showed great sensitiv-ity to the patients and staff at the clinic. He then expounded on the protesters' constitutional right to their freedom of speech. Looking at the evidence, he found that the peaceful demonstra-tion in front of the clinic was well within their rights. The deci-sion would be heralded as supporting a pro-life position.

Rick's words came back to me, *He taught me not to seek the truth, but the truth of the case.*

Before me was a judge who clearly believed in and respected our constitutional system. Rather than basing his decisions on a particular political bent or popular sentiment, he sought a stan-dard of fairness and justice to the parties within the confines of the Constitution and the individual circumstances. No simple label of liberal or conservative would stick to this man.

Sitting in front of the computer screen, digesting the impar-tial legal reasoning, the thoughtful discourse, and the respect extended to all parties across the political spectrum, I knew destiny had knocked on my door. His name was Max Rosenn. He would forever change my life.

> # Justice, justice shall thou pursue.
> —Deuteronomy, 16:20
>
> Verse earmarked by congregation year after year
> for Judge Rosenn to read at synagogue

An Eagle's View

Monte and I were determined to join Judge's final farewell, but we hit a snag. By the time we'd made arrangements for the care of our three young children, no flights would get us from our home in Iowa City to Wilkes-Barre in time for the funeral. Driving through the night gave us our best chance. If we didn't make the funeral, we would at least arrive in time to join a special gathering of the law clerks after the burial.

We chatted across Illinois and into Indiana. In the depths of the night, words became fewer and the music louder. We rolled down the windows to let in the crisp winter air.

We'd spent much of our sixteen-hour drive talking about our mentor. Our walk down memory lane was punctuated with laughter over favorite memories. Traveling through Ohio, I finally drifted off to sleep. While I napped, Monte kept thinking about Judge's wisdom, passion for service, and leadership.

The sun was rising over western Pennsylvania to usher in February 9, 2006, when Monte's excited voice zapped me awake. "Do you realize that knowing Judge was like knowing Thomas Jefferson? Have you *really* thought about the caliber of man he was? He was like one of our country's founding fathers."

I'd never thought of our mentor in this way. Intrigued by his comment, we began a comparison of these two men of uncommon character.

Like Jefferson, Judge was a voracious learner and lifelong student. He was a teacher. He was a diplomat. He was a passionate proponent of self-government and zealous defender of religious freedom. He respected his position of power as a public servant.

When Jefferson penned the Declaration of Independence, he exhibited the rare ability to stand in the place of others, acknowledging it as an expression of the American mind that went far beyond his own. I had watched Judge similarly ponder vast concepts and ideals while paying detailed attention to the impact on individuals of every word he wrote.

Fully awake from the combination of my power nap and this new insight, I offered to take a turn driving. "No, I'm fine," Monte said. "Let's keep going."

As we approached Wilkes-Barre, temporary signs began to appear by the side of the road. They read simply, "Funeral: This Way."

We drove down Franklin Street. Just as we pulled up to the synagogue, the doors opened. Mourners streamed into the bright, cold morning. We had missed the funeral. My heart sank.

Monte and I sat in silence, watching the burgeoning exchange of condolences, handshakes, hugs, tears, and smiles. I picked out Judge's two sons, Keith and Daniel, and their families.

"There's Harold," my husband said quietly, pointing to Judge's brother who had recently arrived from his winter home in California. I spotted him in his black topcoat and hat, accompanied by colleagues from the law firm of Rosenn, Jenkins & Greenwald, which he and Judge had founded.

We had never met a world traveler like Harold before our time in Pennsylvania, and we savored his tales of adventure. Monte's barber once told him that another man was in the shop trying to one-up Harold after nearly every comment he made. The barber said, "OK, let's settle this once and for all. Where is the last place you visited?" Harold replied, "Antarctica." Argument settled.

I couldn't help but smile as I caught a glimpse of white hair and a lanky frame. Joe Savitz endeared himself to me the moment we met when he proudly claimed the title of Judge's first law clerk. He loved telling how he got up the nerve to ask Max Rosenn if he'd be his mentor. Max had recently returned from serving with the army in World War II and was quickly building a reputation as a superb lawyer in the Wyoming Valley, a hotbed for labor relations. Both companies and labor unions respected him for passionately pursuing his client's rights while dispelling the deep distrust and adversarial atmosphere within the labor community.

Max agreed to supervise Joe. A summer clerkship began a friendship that lasted more than sixty years while Joe continued to practice law at the firm founded by his mentor.

I pointed to a man standing among a distinguished-looking group of people. "That's Justice Samuel Alito of the United States Supreme Court." My mentor had sat with Alito on the Third Circuit, the court of last resort for over 25 million people in Pennsylvania, New Jersey, Delaware, and the Virgin Islands. Watching those exiting the synagogue, I picked out judges from all levels of the judiciary who had turned out to honor their respected colleague.

Judge's secretary, Virginia, joined the mourners, wearing her grief on her face. In a recent tribute she had commented, "Every day that Judge Rosenn went to work in the service of the judiciary was a great day for America."

I thought about how Judge was now together again with his wife, Tillie, and his former secretary, Barbara, who had worked by his side for twenty-three years. Both of these women had lost brutal battles to cancer during my clerkship.

More familiar faces joined the group of mourners: the law clerks. A group of once-young lawyers brought together by the solemn occasion, bonded by their love and admiration of one man who inspired them well beyond the year they spent by his side. Deeply molded by their mentor, they went on to become deans of law schools, professors, partners at prestigious law firms, CEOs of multimillion-dollar corporations, top government officials, and bestselling authors.

Each mentorship was a partnership with Judge, rare and beautiful. Clerks reveled in recalling experiences shared with their teacher. Yet the stories and lessons learned were strikingly similar over a span of three decades. Most of us recalled our clerkship as one of the most special years of our life, appreciated even more over time.

My heart-wrenching disappointment over missing Judge's funeral was slowly being eased by wave after wave of awe as I took in the mass procession of his family, friends, colleagues, law clerks, and community members. With an eagle's view, I watched more than seven hundred people stream out of the synagogue as part of a final thank-you to the man who dedicated his life to serving them. Their attendance was a beautiful living testament to our mentor's life, influence, and esteem.

Watching these people, all brought together by a man who lived and breathed community with others, I could hear Judge say: "To give meaning to life, it's important that we help others in need. It is our responsibility to help the next person on the path of life." This man not only walked the path with others; he taught us that this shared path *is* life.

The sacredness of these moments washed over me. I made a silent promise. *Judge, my life has been shaped by you in so many ways. I am a better person for having known you. I promise to use this gift. Other lives will be better for my having been mentored by you.*

═══

I am grateful for that opportunity to have sat in my car with a rare view of the community built by my mentor. Afterward, the Rosenn family graciously shared a firsthand account of how they eulogized and honored their patriarch. These eulogies stirred memories and stories from deep within me.

The stories of my mentor's life are a part of who I am and

who I continue to become. Stories he shared as I worked by his side or over leisurely dinners. Stories shared through dear mutual friends. Most importantly, lessons learned as I simply observed how he lived. For the silent influence of his living example spoke the loudest.

It is common advice to focus on a person's life, not their death. There is wisdom in this. It is not the day we die that defines us, but how we lived.

For many of us, if we received news that we had a specific, limited time left on this earth, we would change course. We would realign the time and energy that flows through our days to the greatest priorities of our life. My mentor was a rare man who lived his life while keeping front and center this truth: each day, we write our eulogy.

It is in his eulogies that you will see the man my mentor was and how he came to be. You will come to understand that our legacy lies in the decisions we make, day in and day out, over the course of our lifetime.

When I was young, I believed that a full life was simply about living a long, healthy one. As I matured, I began to understand that one who lives life fully is not the one who has lived the longest, but the one who loves most deeply and has the richest experiences.

Watching Judge took my understanding to yet another level. He had both fullness of years and fullness of experiences. But it was the fullness of his contribution to his fellow man that defined the quality of his life.

> Helping others in need is
> not only a responsibility of life;
> it is what gives meaning to life.

Wearing Humanity Lightly

Friends and strangers, judges and lawyers, religious leaders and politicians, community members and those who traveled miles joined together with the sole purpose of honoring the man they loved so well.

Light streaming through the stained-glass windows reflected off the golden walls of the synagogue, illuminating the prayer hall. The casket was decorated with a folded flag in recognition of Judge's service in World War II.

It was an appropriate place to say a final farewell. Judge was at the groundbreaking for the synagogue. He and his beloved Tillie were one of the first couples married in it.

Rabbi Meir Rosenberg observed: "Our service is rather austere in nature. I think it reflects the personality of Judge Rosenn." He opened with chanting a psalm in Hebrew, his halting tones rising and falling around the silent congregation. Cantor Ahron Abraham chanted in a deep voice beside him.

The rabbi followed with an English reading: "Praiseworthy is the man that walked not in the counsel of the wicked . . . He shall be like a tree deeply rooted alongside brooks of water that yields its fruit in due season, and whose leaf never withers, and everything he does will succeed."

When Judge was a young man living in Pennsylvania, his grandmother and other members of his family from Hungary were killed in the Holocaust.

In his outer office hung a frame with the Olympic medals from a cousin who lost his life at the hand of the Nazis. His cousin's wife survived, thanks to a Christian coworker using an "Out of Order" sign to conceal her at the library where they worked. For over a year, the Jewish woman read during the day and came out for food at night. The librarian never disclosed to her husband, a general in the Hungarian army, that she was sheltering a Jew for fear that he would turn her over. She ultimately escaped to England, carrying the medals with her, and made arrangements to give them to her husband's family.

On my welcome tour of the chambers as a new clerk, Judge stopped in front of the medals. With a profound look of sadness, he observed: "These are a tangible reminder of the loss of life of a very able, innocent person. He was killed for no reason other than being a Jew. It is difficult to believe that humans could be so cruel and vicious. Taking the lives of 6 million innocent men, women, and children for no good reason whatsoever—but for the sake of power. Exercising power for such evil purposes is unbelievable."

As we continued the tour, he shook his head and quietly remarked, "The Holocaust was barbaric."

Years after my clerkship, I learned that many Jewish prisoners recited a prayer as they were led to their death in the Nazi concentration camps. Naked and without a single material possession, stripped of their status, dearest relationships, and any semblance of a life they once knew, they embraced possessions that no man could take away: faith, free will, and the ability to choose their attitude.

With their final breath, untold numbers of Jewish prisoners chose to speak the *Shema*, giving praise to their God with these words:

> *Hear, O Israel, the Lord is our God*
> *The Lord is One.*

*You shall love the Lord, your
God, with all your heart, and with all your
Soul, and with all your strength.*

*Take to heart these words, which I enjoin on
you today. Drill them into your children. Speak
of them at home and abroad, whether you are busy
or at rest. Bind them at your wrist as a sign and let
them be as a pendant on your forehead.*

*Write them on the doorposts of your houses
and upon your gates.*

Reading this prayer shed light on the faith that my mentor wore as a second skin. In his legal career, he saw cases that highlighted the worst of mankind. He had a front-row seat from which to see the depravity of murderers, rapists, drug dealers, and mafia bosses. Yet, he did not let these experiences cause him to become jaded or cynical. He stood against injustice while carrying his faith in the goodness of man like a torch. He kept hope alive, believing that change was always possible. He created a clean slate with each new case, choosing time and time again to dispense the greatest level of fairness given the law and the situation.

In his personal life, he gently yielded to what life brought him without seeing himself as a victim or complaining about misfortunes. He didn't fall into the trap that many of us do, complaining that life is unfair while failing to complain that this inequality is often in our favor. I never saw Judge entertain that proverbial question of angst that has destroyed hope throughout the ages: "Why me?"

One day he came into my office. "I have some sad news. Mrs. Rosenn has received a diagnosis of pancreatic cancer. It's inoperable. The doctors say she has little time to live. Our concern is to make her as comfortable as possible for the time she has left."

As a newlywed, I couldn't imagine how it would feel to receive such news. Watching Judge support his wife through her illness and prepare for her passage was an incredible journey to learn from. He accepted his lot without any sign of bitterness. He did not spend energy fighting reality but on embracing the whole of his experience as it was.

Watching him continue on without his wife brought additional lessons. While staying connected to the love he shared with Tillie, he set out to discover new layers of love with others. He openly received the support of family and friends. He stayed active, not in an attempt to push away his emotions, but as a way of embracing each day of life that he was being gifted. To his final days, his appreciation for his wife's intelligence, strength of spirit, and character shone brightly.

Through Tillie's illness and death, Judge continued to put out high-quality work and make sure my clerkship was as challenging and enriching as it had been for all of my predecessors. Perhaps I was additionally blessed. For watching him taught me that through the most devastating loss we can choose to focus on and show gratitude for the continued blessings of work, family, health, love, and life. We are free to smile in the midst of trials and laugh in the midst of pain.

His loss reminded me that all things I cherish will fall away. He showed me that we gain strength by letting them go in a spirit of gratitude for having experienced and enjoyed them for the time they were shared.

My mentor experienced enough loss in his life to know that it would not kill him. He experienced enough success to know it would not insulate him from the woes of our human condition. He wore his humanity lightly.

> There is no adversity that cannot bear a gift, and no gift that cannot bring adversity.

Breaking Bread—
With an Apple

Judge's youngest son, Daniel, a pediatric psychologist from Boston, walked to the front of the temple to deliver his eulogy. "I want to thank you for coming here this morning. But more than that, Keith and I want to thank the community for the multitude of 'living' eulogies and tributes Dad was fortunate to receive during his lifetime. To his neighbors, relatives, friends, colleagues, doctors, and especially Virginia and his law clerks, let me express on behalf of the family my deepest gratitude for the caring, concern, and devotion you extended to him.

"Dad's final years were plagued by a deceptive and tricky illness. His rheumatic heart valves began to fail rapidly, and his only

chance was massive open-heart surgery. The surgeon warned against doing any operation, since eighty-five-year-old men do not usually survive this kind of multiple heart valve replacement. I urged the doctor to just talk to Dad for ten or fifteen minutes and then decide."

The mourners laughed knowingly at Daniel's urging of the doctor to take a closer look at his father to get a better sense of who he was dealing with.

"We flew Dad to Boston for a brief meeting with the doctor. After an hour and twenty minutes, the doctor came out to the waiting room and said to me, 'Your dad is so charming and fascinating. He's like a sixty-year-old man. I could have spent the whole afternoon talking to him.'

"The surgery was successful, and Dad thrived for another decade providing incredible contribution, service, and social connection."

"Mollie, I know you thought you'd stay with Judge as long as he's on the bench. But he is eighty-five years old. Surely he'll retire in a year or two."

"You're underestimating Judge's passion for what he does," I said, shaking my head. Monte knew it, too, and was simply grasping at straws, trying to make me feel better.

It had become increasingly clear that this discussion was coming. I waited for the question in each phone call with my mother-in-law. I usually didn't have to wait too long before she asked, "And . . . *when* are you moving back to Iowa?"

Their four-month-old grandson was pulling on their emotions like a magnet to steel. They wanted us closer so they could watch him grow up. It didn't take much pleading to call home their son's heart, a large piece of which had never left. Monte's trips "back home" were becoming more and more frequent, and it took longer for him to adjust to our life in Pennsylvania each time the plane from Iowa touched down.

My soul-searching brought me to the conclusion that my husband would never become a sliver of who he was meant to be if cut off from the oxygen that only Iowa seemed to provide to the core of his being. If our family was going to flourish, it would need to be on the rich soil of the heartland. I was living on borrowed time.

Leaving Judge and my close network of friends would be one of the most difficult decisions of my life. As I prepared to tell him of my decision, my mind floated back to the day he invited me to extend my clerkship beyond the standard one-year term. He had never invited a clerk to extend the term, and it caught me by surprise.

At the time, Monte and I were madly-in-love newlyweds, exploring each other and the whole East Coast one adventure at a time. We were actively involved in the community, serving on various nonprofit advisory boards, participating in the Big Brothers Big Sisters program, and teaching as adjunct professors at local colleges. When we told Judge we'd decided to stay in the area beyond my clerkship, he helped us find the perfect little Cape Cod bungalow nestled in the Pocono Mountains. Life was good. Very good. And it was about to get better.

I excitedly shared my news. "Judge, I was just hired as a litigator at Kreder & Brooks in Scranton."

He knew this was my top choice as a firm that would give me immediate litigation experience. "Congratulations," he said with noticeable approval. "That is a fine firm. I know many of the partners well. I have two clerks coming in next year already, of course. One from New York and the other from Wisconsin. Very upstanding individuals. Both of them."

I smiled at Judge's comment about the integrity of his incoming clerks. Unlike many court of appeals judges who selected clerks only from their alma mater or from the few top law schools, Judge was willing to consider any applicant who came well recommended, particularly from his own son or a former law clerk. He put great thought into his selection of a cadre of very bright, "upstanding" young lawyers and showed pride in their distinguished careers in law, public service, academia, and business.

Judge paused. "I have not made hiring plans beyond that." I caught my breath. Was this conversation really going in the direction it seemed? A quick glimpse of apprehension likely showed on my face.

My mentor smiled with compassion, a look I'd become accustomed to over my year with him. "Mollie, if you would like to return as my clerk after one year of practicing law, I would be honored to have you stay with me as long as I am on the bench."

Normally, I would have responded with my typical, "I'll have to talk this over with Monte," especially when the decision would have such an impact on the life of my family. But the words poured from my heart with a sentiment that I knew my husband would share. "Judge, the honor would be mine."

Two additional years of clerking passed quickly, and it was time for another conversation, one I was approaching with a heavy heart. I stopped outside the door to his chambers to breathe in the sacredness of the space I was about to enter. A space in which Judge conducted his work with the heart of a servant and a deep respect for all the lives he touched through his power.

What a gift it was to be taught as a young professional that stillness was the breeding ground not only of wisdom but also of connection. Years of formal education had taught me that my value came from what I thought and said, not who I was. It seduced me into believing that I had all the answers, or needed to pretend I did.

Judge helped me relearn the truth I knew as a child. It is in comfortable silence that two souls most powerfully connect to the full and complete presence of each other. Each day upon entering these doors, Judge gave me permission to slow down and simply be with him and with myself. The walls of his chambers and his presence whispered: "All is well. Be here with me. Give yourself permission to be with yourself, perhaps for the first time in a long time. *Be still.*"

I softly knocked on the door and stepped in as Judge looked up from his desk. He had been writing letters, a task he savored on a daily basis. While his clerks embraced the growing use of technology over time, he chose never to learn computer skills. He enjoyed the personal connection of handwritten correspondence. Even when he dictated letters for his secretary to type, he often penned a note at the bottom.

"Judge, is this a good time?"

"Of course, Mollie."

Putting down his pen, he shifted his position toward me. As he gave to everyone who walked through these doors, I now had his full attention. I gathered my thoughts, looking down at the gold bar with large block letters on his desk:

E X C E L L E N C E.

He patiently waited for my next words. Looking up into his wise hazel-brown eyes, all I could manage was, "Judge, Monte and I've been talking and . . . well, it's time."

"I see," he said with a look of understanding. "Yes, I knew this day was coming."

I was taken aback by his response, but not surprised. Although I'd never directly mentioned Monte's intent to return home, it apparently had not escaped Judge's keen observation. I was unable to say more.

My inability to speak wasn't fueled by any type of anxiety but rather by a breaking heart. I can't recall ever experiencing anxiety in Judge's presence. As a young lawyer with an inner striving to do and be so much, I spent some nights tossing and turning as uncompleted tasks and unpursued dreams used my mind as their nocturnal playground. But any angst melted away in the presence of Judge, in the stillness of his chambers. My worries evaporated, replaced by a deep contentment that I learned could only flourish when engaging in the present moment.

My mentor not only engaged in the present moment; he masterfully built a life of *sacred moments*, paying as close attention to his inner life and relationships as he did to his work and accomplishments. He taught me that we are architects of our time, moment by moment, one building block at a time.

Judge motioned toward an apple and paring knife on the far corner of his desk. "Would you like to share an apple with me?"

Taking a deep breath, I allowed the stillness of his chambers to settle into my heart. "Yes, I would like that very much."

We sat down together on the dark leather couch. I silently watched as he held the apple in one hand and the knife in the other. The knife sliced through the apple and a trickle of juice ran down the outside of its green skin.

As I reached out to accept the piece of apple he offered, his hand brushed up against mine. "Well, my dear. It's been quite a ride."

For the first time since I walked into his chambers, I smiled. "Yes it has, Judge." Unsure how I would swallow with the large lump in my throat, I took a small bite and savored the tartness. The flavor of the apple mingled with the moment of connection with a man I adored.

"You are doing the right thing. Supporting your husband in this way. I know it's not easy. But I understand if it's best for your marriage." A moment of silence passed. As if agreeing with himself, he said softly: "Monte's a good man. It's the right thing to do."

He cut another piece of apple. Handing it to me, he looked deeply into my eyes. "I do hate to see you go, my dear. It's a sad day indeed."

The wall of tears aching to be released did not fully burst, but they began to trickle down my cheek, mingling salty water with the tartness of the apple. "I know, Judge. I know. And I hate to go. In so many ways, I'm not ready to leave. I still have much to learn from you.

Resorting to the only explanation I could voice without more tears, I softly said, "But, it's time."

He gave a small nod of understanding. "Yes, it is time."

As we nibbled on the apple, I slowly found my voice again. We shared memories of our years together. He affirmed his affection for Monte, and we recalled the too-brief glimpse I had of his marriage and partnership with his beloved Tillie. We laughed at some of our mutual adventures. We discussed highlights of interesting legal cases we had worked on together. We recalled moments of levity experienced with my various co-clerks over the years.

I lost all sense of time as our conversation flowed and memories poured out, swirling around us and settling into the corners of the chambers.

With the apple long finished, Judge assured me that we

would forever share a special connection. "People use telephones and airplanes every day to stay in touch."

Our conversation ended with a lingering hug that said more than any of the words we had managed to voice that afternoon. I walked out of his chambers having shared an apple that had fed my soul as much as it had fed my body. I had broken bread with Judge.

> Your greatest responsibility is to live a life that nourishes your highest truth.

Mentorship Dance

"Dad led as full and complete a life as any man could pray for. Toward the end of his life, he suffered the inevitable losses of the very old: his beloved wife, his devoted sisters, many dear friends, and repeated physical reverses—yet through these all he strode with dignity, courage, and optimism.

"Despite the hardships, he was alert and clear to the very end. This weekend was his ninety-sixth birthday. We gathered in his hospital room—children, grandchildren, great-grandchildren—and sang Happy Birthday. He looked at us and whispered to me, 'I am honored.' Two days later, he died."

When Judge's ninety-fifth birthday was approaching, Monte and I quickly agreed that it would be the perfect occasion for me to fly to Wilkes-Barre and surprise him. For the past few years, I'd treated each visit with Judge as perhaps our last. Although he continued to be strong, as each year passed, the pending reality that he would soon be leaving this earth became clearer.

Judge's secretary, Virginia, happily received news of my scheme and became a gleeful coconspirator. When I walked into his chambers, she greeted me with a warm smile. Putting a finger over her mouth to motion me to be quiet, she pointed toward the law library.

I peeked around the corner. Judge was sitting at the stately conference table, surrounded by books. I stood silently, watching him at work. Memories washed over me.

We'd eaten many lunches at that table, each one like a seminar. We talked about local history, current events, world politics, and literature. Judge commonly brought newspaper clippings that he thought would be of interest. He entertained us with humorous stories, vividly bringing characters to life and teaching lessons.

In the harmonious structure of Judge's day, lunch was used as a break from work. He intentionally arranged his schedule and used his connection with others to fuel his life. He began and ended his time in chambers by personally greeting each person, and he expected us to do the same when we came in after the others. He not only prompted his clerks to exercise daily like him but also arranged gym memberships. Long before power naps were popular, he religiously took a twenty-minute nap each afternoon. He came back to my office between five and six o'clock each day to suggest that it was time to go home to my husband, and then he headed off to enjoy a healthy meal and delight in the company of his fortunate dining companions. My mentor was a master of rejuvenation.

Drafting opinions with Judge at that table was one of the highlights of my clerkship. Examining the legal issues and reasoning never got dull. The variety of cases ranged from criminal proceedings to contract disputes to constitutional protections.

After I prepared a draft of the court's opinion that reflected his rationale, I would sit by his side, going over the decision, word by word. This process produced the well-reasoned, just, and eloquent opinions that were a hallmark of his chambers.

My teacher treated me as an advanced student of the law for whose professional development he was responsible. He gave full consideration to my views, both on the law and on matters of policy. He asked deep and thoughtful questions. He provided a classroom in which this young lawyer not only became a better writer but also learned to adjudicate both the facts and the fair outcome.

In criminal cases, he emphasized that the liberty of a man was at stake. Each year, he took us clerks to visit low- and high-security prisons to put a human face on our work. "The decisions issued from these judicial chambers have a real effect on the lives of people," he reminded us. "Never forget this."

He coupled this protection of individuals with the larger consequence of our decisions. "We must apply the Constitution to protect all Americans from those in positions of power and authority," he would say, "not simply to protect an individual." My teacher felt a duty to do what was right. His was a classroom that nurtured a passion for justice.

It was time to make a new memory at the table. I marched into the law library. "Surprise, Judge! Happy birthday."

"Well, Mollie, this is the second biggest surprise I've had today. The first was when I opened my eyes this morning and realized that I'm still on this earth on my ninety-fifth birthday." His eyes glistened with delight as he stood to embrace me in a bear hug.

I wrapped my arms around him and remembered how, upon meeting him, I'd been surprised by his physical stature, or lack of it. He had a slight frame and stood only five feet seven inches. I very quickly came to see that he was not a man of stature; he was a man of *stature*.

We were so comfortable with each other that it seemed as if I'd seen him only yesterday. We caught up on the major events in our lives and then turned to his birthday celebrations. "My family is holding a dinner this evening to celebrate my birthday," he said. "I would be honored if you would attend as my guest."

He didn't know that his lunch plans had already been decided as well. Under the guise of going out for lunch, we headed toward the courthouse exit. Before we got there, I said: "Judge, I haven't seen the new courtroom. Would you take a minute and give me a tour?" Turning the corner to the courtroom, he was greeted with shouts of "Happy Birthday" from hundreds who gathered in his honor. Not the least bit flustered, he relished the surprise. As I'd seen him do dozens of times, he gave an eloquent thank-you speech, touching the audience with his heartfelt gratitude.

That evening, a more intimate group gathered to celebrate their father, grandfather, and close friend. I sat at a round table directly across from my mentor and spent the evening visiting with his sons, daughters-in-law, and niece. We shared laughs over a clever and entertaining film his grandson produced called

Going to Work with Grandpa, highlighting a day in the life of the judge.

Toward the end of the evening, we were left sitting at the table alone while his family was off thanking their guests. "Well, Mollie," he said as he leaned back in his chair. "You've come all the way from Iowa to celebrate with me."

"How could I not come, Judge?" I asked. "You know what you mean to me."

Without hesitation, he looked deeply into my eyes. "And *you know* what you mean to me."

It was as if these words moved in slow motion as they traveled across the table. Bringing tears to my eyes, they nestled into my heart.

Judge's reply gave me a glimpse of how a mentor is fed by the love and respect of his students. Up to that time, I had viewed my relationship with him more as a one-way street in which he did the giving and I did the receiving. A seed had been planted.

=====

As part of my preparation for writing this book, I signed up to attend an authors' conference in Philadelphia, the same city where Judge and I created many special memories when attending court sittings. The conference offered an option to bring a second guest for a small fee, and an aspiring author I'd recently befriended came to mind. Kelley would benefit from the conference and would appreciate the financial support. I called her and mentioned the upcoming event.

"We think alike!" Kelley exclaimed. "I printed out the entire sales letter to read tonight before I go to bed. I need to figure out a way to get to that conference!"

"You're in."

"What?"

"You're in . . . as my guest. I've paid your fee. You can stay with me in my room. We'll have a slumber party."

"We're going to Philadelphia!"

On the first day of the conference, a man named Henry approached me during a break. He struck me as immensely wise, and left me feeling that our visit was too brief. On the last day of the conference, he invited me to lunch.

After listening to my description of this book, Henry observed, "What a wonderful day it will be when you get to the end of your life and get to see how much light you brought into Judge's life."

"Oh, no. You have that wrong. I was the one who received from Judge."

I'm not sure if the twinkle in Henry's eyes or his smile was brighter. "With time, you're going to see the *full* truth of your relationship." In that moment, the memory of Judge's comment at his birthday dinner flashed into my mind: *And you know what you mean to me.* I then recalled how he often commented, "Friendship is a two-way street." Perhaps so was mentoring.

Later that day, it was time for Kelley to return home. We said a tender good-bye. I had brought her to Philadelphia to support her development as an author. She had become one of my greatest cheerleaders to complete this book.

We'd spent hours talking about the lessons Judge taught me. "He inspired me to know that wherever life takes me, I am made for more. In a world that accepts mediocrity and idolizes comfort, I have a responsibility to listen to how I'm being called to become more and to serve more. This invitation will continue until the day I die."

Her words took my breath away. "Mollie, this book is part of your *more*. You must write it."

Not yet ready for the quiet of an empty room, I stopped by the hotel restaurant to process our time together over a cup of tea. When I returned to the room, I found a note on my bed.

Mollie,
For as much as you are, for as much as you've learned and
seen (as a wise person once told me. . .) Become More.
Thanks for finding me, my beautiful sister.

The next morning, I found another note in my toiletry bag:

You're amazing. Shine on.

Once I had settled into my seat on the airplane, I cracked open a book given to me by a literary agent I'd met at the conference who expressed interest in representing this book. Out fell another note:

The Judge will come to life again through you and inspire
so many others. You must write his story.

The image of Judge honoring me at his ninety-fifth birthday celebration blended with the note I held in my hand. Henry's voice joined in, confidently suggesting that one day I would fully see the happiness I brought to my mentor's life. A small drop of understanding grew in its richness, allowing my mind and heart to more fully entertain ways in which Judge received from me.

As my mentorship of others has grown over time, I more fully understand the delicate two-way street between teacher and student. There exists a yin and yang of mentorship, a breathing in and out.

A strong mentor, in a spirit of humility, fosters an understanding in the student of the give-and-take of the relationship. A wise student pulls her focus back from all she is receiving and musters up great courage to acknowledge the ways in which she enriches her mentor.

Kahlil Gibran writes of a bee and a flower. The flower gives life to the bee while the bee gives love to the flower. This is the dance of mentorship.

> A wise teacher learns in the midst of teaching; a wise student teaches in the midst of learning.

Hospital Justice

"In the last few years, I tried to persuade Dad to come up to Boston and live with us. The offer was genuine, but his response was known long before the offer was made. We all knew, his doctors better than anyone, that he would never give up. His legal career sustained him and literally kept him alive.

"Last year, during another health crisis, Dad was lying in the ICU hooked up to cardiac monitors. I could see on the screen above his head as I was talking with him just how irregular and rapid his heart rate was. And then Keith began discussing with him one of Dad's legal decisions. To my astonishment, his rapid rate slowed and his rhythm dramatically improved. It was like the healing power of the law literally flowed into his bloodstream.

"A few weeks ago, when Dad and I discussed the ending of life, *he told me he was not ready to die yet. He still had several more decisions to finish."*

Joe Savitz walked into the hospital intensive care unit, thinking about how Virginia had let the cat out of the bag during their phone conversation. Judge, who had been hospitalized with a bout of pneumonia, had been getting out of bed to work on opinions. His two law clerks were on the run, carrying books and drafts of court opinions back and forth between chambers and the hospital every day.

He dictated notes to send his colleagues, telling them he was keeping up with everything. The previous week he'd instructed Virginia by phone: "My panel is sitting next week. Please call the chief judge and ask her to set up a videoconference."

She had never told Judge no before. Even though he treated her with the respect due to his equal, she clearly understood the boundaries that came with their relationship. But given his health condition, his request went too far. She laid down the law for the first time. "Judge, no way."

Her boss agreed not to do the conference but continued to pour his energy into the work he loved. She called Joe to help reinforce her attempts to slow down his work pace.

Joe rounded the corner into the hospital room. He stopped short. Despite Virginia's warning, he was surprised to see his friend sitting in a lounge chair in front of a table, documents and books spread out before him.

"Max! What are you doing out of bed?"

"What do you think I'm doing? I'm working on an opinion. I'm not going to sit in bed. I'm better off working in a chair. And these opinions have to get out!"

"You need to slow down. Virginia called and told me that you got an opinion out from the hospital."

Judge slowly shook his head.

Confusion showed on Joe's face. "What? She said you've had your law clerks up here every day and that you finished an opinion."

Judge slowly shook his head from side to side again.

Joe stood speechless, trying to make sense of his earlier discussion with Virginia.

Then, with a glint his eye, Judge held up six fingers.

It took Joe a moment to grasp its meaning. Not one opinion, but six!

This was the work ethic that made Max Rosenn one of the most respected icons in the legal and judicial community. He spent his ninetieth birthday on a three-judge panel, hearing a case on sentencing guidelines. At ninety-five years of age, he still traveled to Philadelphia to hear court cases. Just a few months before his death, when featured in the Pennsylvania public television documentary "Max Rosenn: An Uncommon Conscience," he gave a rousing, passionate speech to a full house on constitutionalism and the Guantánamo Bay detention camp.

The six lengthy judicial opinions that he completed from his hospital room during the last couple of weeks of his life would be published in the federal reporters after his death.

A few days after Joe's visit, Judge lost his ability to talk. His sons and their families had come to town in preparation for his ninety-sixth birthday. The plan was to hold a party at the local Westmoreland Club, a historic and elegant Georgian mansion in downtown Wilkes-Barre. With their father in the hospital, there was talk about not having the party.

Judge would have none of this. He motioned for a pen and pad of paper. "The party goes on," he wrote. "Make sure everyone has a good time."

> Mastery is the breeding ground of fresh, creative passion.

The Making of a Lawyer

"We knew that Dad would never leave the Wyoming Valley that he loved so much. He said to me last Passover, 'I was born here and this is where I lived my life. This is where I'll end my time.'

"Dad was born in his mother's bed in a ramshackle house in Midvale, just about a mile from where he died. The oldest of five children, he was parentified and adultified almost from the start. His mother, my Grandma Jen, used to tell the story of how she had a birthday party for him with some neighborhood kids when he turned six. Midway through the party, she had to run down to the store for more soda. When she got back, she found Max had sent everyone home because they were too noisy and they were misbehaving."

A ripple of laughter echoed throughout the synagogue. It was *not too difficult to imagine the eminently proper Judge Rosenn being born "an old man."*

My mentor had a courtliness and formality about him. His sister used to elfishly whisper to the clerks, "Judge has a rubber necktie that he wears in the shower." Daniel recalled, "My Dad's formality often led my young cousins to address him as Uncle Mr. Max."

Law clerks from over three decades share the moment when they were called to put on their work clothes to help do some sort of manual labor. The clerks showed up in jeans or sweats, carrying their work gloves. Our boss inevitably showed up wearing "an old suit and tie." In response to the look of surprise on his clerks' faces, he simply replied, "What? You have your work clothes, and I have mine."

His formal style of dress and behavior didn't feel stuffy, though. His high standards simply reflected the respect with which he viewed his position. He never wanted to do anything that invited a disregard for the law.

In conversations with my mentor, I'd see pieces of how he was shaped by the responsibilities he bore as the oldest child. As a young boy, he saw one brother die. He looked after his other three siblings, putting them to bed nearly every night while his father traveled through cattle country and his mother worked at their family grocery store. While still a child, he took on banking tasks at the store and kept busy on the farm looking after the cattle.

Each of his parents influenced his decision to become a lawyer, but in very different ways. Joe Rosenn had an intense interest in public speaking. A good speech of any nature drew him in like a bug to a light on a dark night. He spent hours at the courthouse listening to lawyers argue cases. If an able attorney was addressing a jury, Joe found a way to be there, and he took his oldest son with him.

When Max was fourteen years old, his father had a burning desire to attend the 1924 National Democratic Convention in New York City. A lack of invitation was not going to stop him. It was a day that would forever remain in his son's memory: "The first day of the convention, I spent as much time watching the look of awe on my father's face as I did watching the elegant and persuasive speakers."

On the second day of the convention, they could not get into the hall without a pass. Being turned away at the door did not faze Joe. Up he climbed over the fire escape of Madison Square Garden. Up Max went right after him. They entered the auditorium through the fire escape, took a seat, and spent the rest of the day listening to speeches. Max learned a lot that day from the man sitting next to him, who was not intimidated by anything or anyone.

Ironically, Joe had a strong desire in later years to have his son forgo college to help him in his cattle business. It was too late. He had already set in motion his son's strong interest in the law and advocacy.

It was Judge's mother, Jennie, who served as his greatest ally in becoming a lawyer. She was passionate about education. Although it was not customary for first-generation immigrants to send their children to college, she insisted that all of her children attend college, even the girls. Though Joe couldn't see the sense in this, she made clear to him that no argument would be entertained. Through the enormous financial pressures their family faced during the Great Depression, it was Jennie who determinedly insisted that her son finish law school. Judge carried these lessons forward, instructing his own sons: "You can always lose your money. You can never lose your education."

One seemingly normal day of taking care of cattle when he was nine years old, my mentor had an experience that stood out as the time he first knew that his life would be inextricably connected with the law.

He and another boy were taking a few cattle to the pasture to graze. One of the animals was a young heifer. As they were crossing the road, a sports car came along. It was a green Chandler—a small, open touring car.

The driver had a good view and saw the boys and the cattle, but he was driving carelessly. He ran down the heifer, broke its leg, and kept on going. Max caught sight of the license number, but he didn't have anything to write with. He kept repeating the number to himself over and over in order to memorize it. They continued to the pasture with the cattle, including the wounded heifer.

When they got to the pasture, Max took the stick that he used to drive the cattle and wrote the license number in the dirt. He then sent the other boy to go get his father. When Joe arrived, his son told him what had happened.

"Did you get the license number?" his father asked.

"Yes, I did."

"Where is it?" Max pointed to the ground where he had written the number.

With a look of disbelief, Joe immediately called the state police, who verified that the plate matched the number of a green Chandler. They apprehended the driver, who was arrested and brought before a magistrate.

The magistrate held a hearing. Young Max was the chief witness—the only witness. He identified the car, the color, and told exactly what had happened. The car owner denied that he was in the accident, but the magistrate believed the boy. The driver was ordered to fully compensate Joe Rosenn for the damages to his calf.

A competent, credible, and unflappable nine-year-old witness got his first taste of justice being administered through the legal system, ending with the culprit paying for his misdeed.

Just as the tallest redwood tree starts from a tiny seed, this experience planted a seed within my mentor. It fell on fertile ground. His parents' interests in advocacy and education would nurture the young boy to grow into one of the most prolific jurists and strongest legal pillars in America.

> With every choice you create the life you'll live; with every decision you design it.

A Man of the People

"Dad didn't go to public school until he was eight, and he quickly made up for lost time. He entered Cornell University when he was only sixteen and the University of Pennsylvania Law School just three years after that. He was always incredibly focused, goal-directed, and motivated. His mother instilled in him a love of education and that's something he passed on to his family.

"Dad's mother also instilled in him the need to treat everyone with dignity. He was the epitome of a small-town person, in the very best sense of the word. He seemed to know everyone in the valley.

"Walking with him from the courthouse to the Westmoreland Club for lunch was an exercise in stopping and starting. Every few steps he would turn to greet one person and then another.

"He had a phenomenal memory not just for names and faces,

but also for lineage. He would introduce me to an elderly lady, and when she left, he would tell me what town down the river her family came from and to whom her mother was married."

When Max was a boy, hobos frequently visited his home and asked for a contribution. These men were respectfully known as *mendicants* in his home. One man scared him a bit. He came down to their home from Scranton, about twenty miles to the north. He would knock on the door and in a high nasal tone ask for money. His mother always said yes.

"No one can refuse to give aid and assistance to their fellow man because they are poor and don't have the money," Jennie instructed her sons. "There are always people poorer than you, so even though you may be poor, you've got to assist your fellow man. If someone comes asking for money, give them one dollar no matter what, no questions asked."

One day, five-year-old Max was playing. His aunt, known for her generous spirit, was visiting from out of town. He heard his mother say to her sister, "Look out the window and see what's happening."

Max joined them at the window and saw the hobo from Scranton in the yard picking up his mother's clothespins. They peered out the window for a couple of minutes watching the man collect the clothespins. He headed toward the front of their house. Jennie answered the knock on her door.

"Would you like to buy some clothespins today?" asked the man.

"Yes, I would," replied Jennie. "How much are they?"

"I have six clothespins. That will be fifty cents."

"Wait a minute while I go get some change."

As Jennie went to get money, her sister vehemently opposed her decision. "Jennie, why would you do such a thing? Those are your clothespins. Have you lost your mind? You're not going to buy your own clothespins!"

"No," said Jennie. "That man needs our help and deserves our respect. If he wants to retain a little bit of dignity and sell me my clothespins, I'm not going to complain. I would have given him the money anyway. This way he has some dignity left, and I'm pleased to do it."

Young Max learned a lesson about respect that day. A lesson he never forgot.

Jennie was a responsible and industrious woman, born the tenth of twelve children to an orthodox Jewish family in Hungary. At the age of sixteen, she packed up her meager possessions and sailed to America. When she married in her early twenties, she opened a butcher shop attached to their home. Over time, it grew into a full grocery and meat market. People in the community came to rely upon her judgment, her honesty, and her deep sense of compassion. She developed a reputation for never refusing a request for help.

Jennie placed greater emphasis on the values and obligations to society taught by her religion than on religious obligations. She believed that everyone was entitled to his or her views, and she helped people of all different nationalities and faiths. In addition to her native Hungarian and Yiddish, she learned English, Polish, Slavic, and Russian through her interactions with others. Her community dubbed her "a woman of the people."

Her son watched others come to her for counseling, social services, medical help, and legal assistance. When a worker was injured in the mines, his comrades came straight to Jennie to get a doctor. Dying men entrusted her with their life's savings, asking her to send the money back to Europe for them. Despite numerous robberies, she refused to be intimidated and continued to help those in need.

During the coal strike of 1925, long before public assistance existed, hundreds of men were out of work. Max watched his mother borrow money from a local bank to buy merchandise while she carried these families on her books for months. Not caring that it deprived her of profits, Jennie taught them how to be resourceful, making soup from a cheaper bone and using meat substitutions. She did the same with people who rented homes from her during the Great Depression, teaching them how to save money. She went years without raising rent, instead asking renters to work with her to maintain the house they occupied.

As an adult, Judge took up residence near his mother and visited her every day. Decades after his mother's death, my mentor described her as the most influential person in his life. "She helped form my character and shape my destiny. I credit her with my value system. She was a model of hard work and obligations to family and community."

Through her example, Jennie taught her children that helping others less fortunate wasn't simply a good or charitable thing to do, it was the just thing to do. It was righteous.

In turn, Judge taught his clerks that as part of humanity, we have a sacred obligation to make the world a better place. He showed us that the path to a full and meaningful life is through giving. The more we give from our heart of our time, talent, money, and selves, the richer we become.

My mentor was a rare man who didn't choose between

investing his money or investing himself in a charitable project. He invested in his community wholly. He gave time, money, and himself to further his greatest priorities. There was no gap between his professed values and his true values. He lived as he believed. In one word, Judge taught *stewardship*.

From the first day of my clerkship, he emphasized that the gifts and the support I'd received on the way to become his clerk—including my intelligence, education, experience, legal skills, talents, health, and relationships—had been given to share. He built in opportunities to be of service through the local bar association and community organizations. He encouraged me to find my own ways to contribute to a more just, fair, and equitable society.

He instilled in me—no, he *inspired me* to live from—a place of making a conscious choice on a daily basis to share my blessings with others. Why? Simply because I could.

No clerk left the side of Judge Rosenn without having learned this lesson: You have both the right and the responsibility to be a faithful steward of the blessings you have in your life. This choice is made through your actions. Be generous in your giving.

My mentor taught me that degrees and accolades would never determine my worth as a leader. They only brought a higher standard of responsibility to serve one's community for the common good. A leader's true value is created by the compassion and healing he or she brings to humanity.

Judge's mother so greatly influenced him that from time to time he mentioned thoughts of writing a book about her. I don't know all of the stories he would tell. From the ones I heard, they would be stories of charity, respect for others, and being worthy of the trust of one's neighbor. He would write about how she taught him to walk in integrity, help the poor, seek justice, and defend victims of oppression. He would credit her for showing him the value of learning and passionately embracing the value of education for all. He would thank her for her example of being brave in the face of adversity and mild mannered in dealing with others.

My mentor never got around to writing that book about his mother. Yet, all who knew him experienced a living testament to the lessons she taught him. For when he talked about this servant of the people, he easily could have been talking about himself.

> As part of humanity, each of us
> is called to develop and share
> the unique gifts we are given.

Calm Waters Run Deep

"Dad was never interested in running for office, but he truly liked people. And they liked him. He somehow engendered respect wherever he went.

"He never exaggerated or bragged. He was always in control. In all my life, I never knew him to really lose his temper. He never swore or told an off-color story.

"When he spoke, he neither understated nor overstated. He simply told the truth. He said what he thought.

"He himself was a marvelous listener—very alert, quizzical, and inquiring."

It was April 1992, and Judge and I were leaving Philadelphia to return home to Wilkes-Barre after a few days of sitting with the court. Although we clerks usually did the driving, he decided to drive out of the city because he felt more comfortable driving when rush hour traffic was especially heavy.

As we worked our way out of Philadelphia, Judge went to make a quick change of lanes. He didn't see the car in his blind spot to our right, and the cars collided. Lurching forward, he hit his head on the rearview mirror. I recovered from the initial jolt to see a stream of bright red blood flowing down the side of his face.

The other driver followed us off the path of traffic. We checked that she wasn't injured, and Judge provided his insurance information. Her car was not badly damaged, so she drove away as we settled in to wait for an ambulance.

Judge rested leisurely against a tree in the median. The white handkerchief he held to his head turned a bright crimson as blood flowed from the deep gash. Yet, he sat quietly, as if he were enjoying a respite amid the snarled traffic.

In the ambulance, he chatted with me, taking the focus off himself and asking about my well-being. At the hospital, he turned his attention to conversation with the doctor stitching up his head. He never once lost his calm demeanor.

Years later, Virginia told me how Judge had suffered a

mini-stroke while sitting in the library. His left side went numb. She gripped his hands, checked the size of his pupils, and asked a few questions. She then called the U.S. Marshals who provided courthouse security to escort Judge and her to the hospital.

The emergency staff stabilized him. After changing his medications, he made a prompt recovery. Virginia recalled, "The whole time, his eyes showed no fear, just curiosity and the expectation that I would fix it, whatever it was." This is how Judge led. He approached whatever life brought with a fierce curiosity. He hired people who could do the job and calmly communicated his full trust in their ability to handle whatever circumstances arose.

Some of us are born with a cooler disposition. Others need to work to grow our ability to calmly handle what comes our way. In writing this book, I asked those who knew him if Judge had a temper as a younger man. I thought that perhaps he had learned to regulate it by the time I met him.

It seems that he was always pretty even-keeled. The worst bit of dirt I found came from his law firm secretary. When the young lawyer became annoyed by something she'd done, he looked her straight in the eye and, with a note of exasperation, exclaimed, "I hope your husband eats crackers in bed!"

Rosenn clerkships were punctuated with epiphanies, as our eyes were opened to how the simple act of listening fuels justice. First, listen. Then ask questions.

One of my favorite justice epiphanies blessed clerk Jonah Zimiles, who fondly refers to it as "Conscious in St. Croix." He traveled with Judge to St. Croix, Virgin Islands, in the early 1980s to hear oral arguments. One of the functions performed by the panel was to discipline court personnel allegedly responsible for delays in the judicial system. The proceedings had been so hostile in the past that the presiding chief judge traveled incognito in the Virgin Islands because he feared being attacked by the locals.

A wayward employee's name was called. The clerk of court glowered at him with disapproval. He approached the bench as if facing a death sentence. The presiding judge immediately rebuked him, giving a tongue-lashing for being behind in producing court transcripts. The other judges on the panel sat silently.

Judge Rosenn suddenly interceded. "Is there a reason why you are behind with the transcripts?"

Sensing Judge's compassion, the young man launched into a moving speech. He told Judge that a lack of proper equipment and training had impeded his work, so he had bought new equipment and taken a special course at his own expense. He explained how he had decreased his backlog notwithstanding an increasingly burdensome caseload. He quietly concluded, "I have worked nights and weekends, neglecting my family in an attempt to catch up. I pray daily for the strength to serve the court."

As the embarrassed presiding judge squirmed sheepishly, Judge Rosenn thanked the employee and told him that the court now understood the situation.

This is the type of lesson learned working alongside a man who resonated with strength and kindness, calm confidence and humility. He showed that these attributes are not in conflict, but come together to create justice.

> Every person is a living treasure box.
> Listening holds the key.

Gifts and Presence

"My dad had a presence—it's hard to describe—an aura of poise and quiet authority. He was a leader. People turned to him for advice, and they relied on him.

"When I was in fourth grade, in the midst of polio season, I saw a movie about a child being treated in an iron lung, the artificial breathing device of the day. This put a great and real fear of polio in my heart. This vision stayed in my mind for days as I worried that I might contract the disease.

"I kept the terror to myself, but eventually I became so frightened about spending my life in an iron lung that I had trouble sleeping and eating. It only took a few words from my protector to make that fear go away.

"When my father learned of my fear, he consoled me and calmly said, 'You don't have to worry about that anymore.' And miraculously, I didn't. When Dad said something, you could always believe him. His strength and his composure protected our family and kept us from worry."

"What is the greatest lesson you learned from the judge?"

This is the question I am asked most frequently about my mentor. And it's a difficult question to answer. He changed how I show up in this world, how I contribute to this world, and what I want for this world.

If I had to narrow his lessons down to the one that had the most impact on me, it would be this: be fully present with others. It may sound simple, but the effects are vast, like a domino setting in motion a long string of dominoes. Judge took the time to look for the best in others and communicated a strong belief that they would live up to his positive vision of what was possible. He affirmed people.

My mentor appeared to have time for every person he interacted with. He looked others right in the eye and showed a genuine interest in what they had to say. He replied in a way that made them feel heard and important. He made them feel good about what they did and who they were. When it was time to part ways, he'd often depart with a gentleman's tip of his hat as a final sign of courtliness and respect.

From years of observing him, I concluded that this wasn't a skill that took conscious effort on his part. He wasn't concentrating on ignoring the noise and distractions around him. He simply had a practice of dropping into a space of love and respect for his fellow man, which ran to his core.

Every time Judge laid eyes on someone, he *saw* them and made a choice to be with them fully in however many moments they would share. It's as if he whispered into the heart of each person he met, "*When I am with you, I am with you.*"

Walking down the street or presiding in a court of law, he showed me time and time again how real connection could open one's eyes—and heart—to consider the viewpoint of the "other side." I witnessed how this connection spread joy to others and strengthened his community with waves of mutual respect.

Judge had a way of observing an apparently mundane detail of life to reveal its truth as a piece of glorious art. The American writer Henry Miller remarked, "The moment one gives close attention to anything, even a blade of grass, it becomes a mysterious, awesome, indescribably magnificent world in itself." My mentor did this not only with the world around him but also with people. He fully saw the beauty of each individual. His focus enriched others.

Judge's engagement in the present moment tapped an ongoing source of humor and appreciation for daily life. Adults and children alike responded to his presence. Long before I was a parent, I watched him warm up my extremely shy six-year-old niece over dinner when her family visited Pennsylvania. Leaving the restaurant, she reached out her little hand to tuck into his and began to skip down the street.

Years later, I experienced the joy of watching him play with my own children. He reveled in buying them simple toys in anticipation of their visits. He lit up as they walked in the door, greeting them with a smile as he lowered himself to their eye level. Inevitably, he'd end up sitting on the floor in chambers, playing games and making them giggle with delight.

The Jewish people have a unique word for the proper mind-set for prayer: *kavanah*.

In kavanah, your mind is free from other thoughts. You bring deep feeling to the meaning of the prayer. The minimum level of this mind-set is an awareness that you are speaking to God with an intention to fulfill the obligation to pray. Any less is considered merely reading, not praying.

My mentor brought this mind-set of mindful living to every interaction with another human being. Conversing with Judge was prayer in motion.

The utmost form of respect is to give sincerely of your presence.

Faith, Hope, and Love

"Dad's life was inextricably bound up with the valley. He met my mother across the river from here at Kirby Park playing tennis when he was sixteen. She was the only woman in his life, and he loved her with a deep, abiding, idealizing love."

Choking back tears, Daniel noted: "He was married right here, behind me. They were inseparable, and her love for him sustained and steadied and completed him. The single most irrepressible sadness of his long life was that she slipped away from him in 1992.

"After Mom's death, Dad seemed to mellow. To me, he seemed more accessible and took on to himself a softer, more nurturing role with his children and grandchildren. It was as if in some way he had internalized Tillie's ineffable motherliness and made this a part of himself."

In a very short time with the Rosenns, it became obvious who ran not only the house but also Judge's heart. I first met Tillie at the door of their beautiful lakefront cottage on Harvey's Lake, a local resort area. My co-clerk and I accepted an invitation to help winterize the cottage and then share a meal. A small compact woman only five feet tall and with glistening blue eyes warmly welcomed us into her home.

We were visiting in the living room when Judge walked in. Tillie stopped mid-sentence. "Oh, Mac," she said, surprising me with her pet name for her husband. "What are you still doing wearing your good suit? You know I need you to help get the house ready for winter!"

As Judge immediately busied himself taking apart a lamp, his wife's attention came back to us. "Excuse my outburst girls, but sometimes . . . well, men can be such boys!"

Tillie's hallmark blend of chutzpah and kindness was readily apparent throughout that lovely night on the lake as she conversed and doted on us. Watching the Rosenns together gave Monte and me great hope as newlyweds. They shared a rare and beautiful love, and they provided us with an ideal to strive for while doing what was best for our lives. Their marriage lit a fire in us to become better people as individuals and as a couple.

Photos of Tillie as a young woman decorated the chambers.

Snapshots captured moments of the active lives they lived together, swimming by their summer cottage, playing golf, and enjoying annual vacations around the world. Looking at her photo one day, Judge commented, "I was initially attracted to my wife's beauty and charm. Over time I've grown an appreciation for her character, her values, and other more permanent and enduring attributes." Without directly telling me what was important in my relationship with Monte, he told me.

Their love and admiration were mutual. Daniel recalled, "Mom was committed to Dad. She believed in him. She said to us, never forget that you are Max Rosenn's son."

After Tillie was diagnosed with pancreatic cancer, I spent many hours visiting her at their home. One Sunday, I sat by the side of her bed holding her hand. Her courage touched me deeply. Through her pain, she exhibited warmth, grace, and humor. Leaning over to kiss her forehead, I whispered, "I love you, Mrs. Rosenn." I looked up to see tears in Judge's eyes. Those were my last words to her.

The memorial service drew clerks from near and far. Story after story of Tillie's support of her husband left no doubt that the love and care she'd given him over the years was the wind beneath his wings. His equal in intellect, generosity, kindness, and insight into human nature, she inspired him to be a better man.

Clerks laughed about how she ended one reunion where they had repeatedly flattered her husband, saying, "Great. What do I do with this giant pancake now that you've got him all dripping with syrup?"

Rosenn clerks adored her as their ally in keeping Judge in line when his personal advice went beyond his area of expertise. The responsibility he felt for his clerks' lives led our mentor to opine on a wide variety of matters, including decorating apartments, proper nutrition, exercise, and most famously finding "appropriate" mates, or at least dates for his available clerks. It was Tillie who stepped in like no other, with a wink toward the clerks, saying, "Oh, Mac, leave those kids alone."

In graduate school, years after my clerkship, I learned that a key indicator of a healthy marriage is the tendency of the partners to recall in vivid detail how they met and to share positive stories of their early days together. I thought of Judge and Tillie.

Judge once said, if given a day of his life to live over again, he'd choose his wedding day. "Although it was a day that rained and was cold and damp, it was the happiest day of my life. It marked the beginning of a long romance that brought joy to myself and many others."

The story of his romance was one I'd heard often over the years. By the time he was eighteen, he and his girl, Tillie Hershkowitz, were quite serious. But he was focused on his education and did not expect this popular and good-looking young lady to wait for him while he attended law school. She waited.

On October 29, 1929, known as Black Tuesday, the stock market imploded following a decade of great prosperity. America experienced an air of desperation and hopelessness never before seen. With no government safety net in place, millions became unemployed. Factories closed. Homes foreclosed left and right. Max's family joined the thousands who lost their home and nearly everything they had, except the resolve to pay their debts and go on with their lives.

He graduated from law school in the spring of 1932, still in the depths of the Great Depression. He very much wanted to marry his love, but a man did not marry if he could not support his wife. He could see Tillie had other suitors, so he told her not to wait for him. She waited.

The twenty-two-year-old lawyer began his solo practice. A year later, he still couldn't afford a ring. With little money but a great desire to marry the woman who held his heart, he accepted his mother's offer of a diamond from a piece of her jewelry. Off he went to the jewelers to mount the stone on a setting for his future bride.

One Friday in March 1933, the jeweler called and told Max that the ring was ready. It was the same day President Roosevelt announced the closing of all banks in America. "I remember the night I proposed to Tillie with crystal clarity, not only because she was the love of my life but also because I was so discouraged about the conditions that confronted us. It felt as if the world was collapsing around us.

"I walked home that night, telling myself what a fool I was to promise to marry a woman and support her when the whole country was declining into nothingness. I didn't know whether the banks would open again on Monday or whether I would have work again or what would happen."

With a sheepish grin and a glint in his eye, he added, "It was one of the smartest things I ever did."

> Hope finds its fulfillment
> when nurtured through faith
> and shared with love.

Prayers Big and Small

"Along with his family and his legal career, Dad's private religious beliefs were a central, organizing force in his life. This went beyond his service to the Jewish community, organizations, and charities he served and frequently led.

"In his civic responsibility, he demonstrated an ideal of commitment to philanthropic giving and charity, which was often non-sectarian.

"Dad loved the traditional values and observances of Judaism, and he lived his life according to them. He said morning prayers, kept Kosher, and went to temple every Saturday that he was able to. He saw a central Truth in the biblical heritage of ancient Israel and the Mosaic Code. It was not necessarily the concept of the Jewish

God, but the principles, the interlocking of community, personal integrity, and duty."

Judge prominently displayed a Hebrew prayer in his chambers that spoke of love, compassion, forgiveness, sharing, beauty, life, truth, and justice. I read it some days, reflecting on how my boss moved daily to these words.

When my friend Bob Burg, coauthor of *The Go-Giver*, told me of five questions his Jewish father asked him as a young boy, it reminded me of the prayer in Judge's chambers.

Bob's father expected him to know the answers to these questions. The first four came from a Jewish sage, and his father added a fifth question:

Who is a rich person? One who rejoices in their lot.

Who is wise? One who learns from all others.

Who is mighty? One who can control their own emotions, and make of any enemy a friend.

Who is honored? One who honors others.

Who is brave? One who is smart enough to be afraid and still do their job.

I could easily imagine my mentor learning similar verses as

a child, and it brought back memories of my own childhood prayers. As a young girl raised in a devout Catholic household, I heard my parents recite a prayer each morning at the breakfast table. I don't remember all the words, but one line has remained over time. Decades later, I say it as part of my own morning ritual. "I offer up my prayers, works, joys, and sufferings of this day."

From a very young age, I understood that this prayer was said as a morning offering. A giving of everything we were and everything we would experience during the day. I was taught through this prayer that life is not fair. It brings sufferings along with the joys. Work is an inherent part of our human condition. It is through work that we use our unique gifts and make a contribution to the well-being of others.

When I was preparing for my First Communion, I needed to memorize certain prayers. One day I was sitting at the counter, reciting them to my mom. She was standing at the stove, stirring a big pot of spaghetti. Cooking for our family of fifteen involved a lot of time standing in front of massive pots and pans at a hot stove.

It dawned on me that one of the first things I heard in the morning was the offering prayer, and I routinely heard my parents saying prayers from their bedroom at night, but I didn't often hear my mom pray during the day.

"Mom, do you pray during the day?"

She looked up from stirring our dinner and laughed. "Honey, do you think I love to cook and do laundry and all of the other chores I do throughout my days? My *whole day* is a prayer."

Like my mom, my mentor offered up each of his daily tasks as a prayer. He was a man who shone with the presence of the divine. Each day, he asked God to be with him as he dedicated himself to carrying forth all of the responsibilities he felt he was being called to execute.

Along with the structured prayers of his faith, Judge said a simple prayer each morning of his adult life. It went like this: "God, help me make a contribution to a just and peaceful world."

The Lord heard his prayer and partnered with Max Rosenn to use him as an instrument of peace and justice to his people. *Amein. Amen.*

> Allow the way to your great work to be guided by your service to others.

A Matter of Faith

"Dad took a deeply personal pride in the historical insights of Judaism and the sacrifices his people made through the ages to keep themselves and their beliefs alive. Although he was always an incredibly rational and analytical man, he kept the traditional observances as best he could in the complicated secular world he lived in.

"It was not the absolutism of Judaism and its observances that intrigued my dad but rather the organicity of the written Commandments.

"The Torah, which to him was the birthplace of our U.S. constitutional law he so revered, was interpreted and explained through the ages by a learned body of rabbis who weighed and construed the laws according to a just and humanistic understanding of God and man. This is where his religion and his legal career came together."

Once while Monte and I were enjoying one of our frequent dinners with him at the East Mountain Inn near our home, Judge asked, "If your faith allowed women to be ordained priests, you would have been one, wouldn't you?"

We hadn't been talking about religion or philosophy or our political views. Yet, his question was delivered casually, as if he were simply asking if I were going to order dessert.

Virginia Woolf writes about shocks of memory. "Moments of being" when we get jolted out of our everyday complacency to see the world in a new way. This was one of those moments. The question caught me off guard; it took my breath away. "Perhaps," I said. What this question represented to me was too big and personal to delve into.

That moment is as real to me today as when I was sitting across the table from Judge. I can see the décor of the Wildflowers restaurant. I can hear the sounds of clinking dishes and utensils around me. I can smell the warm bread in front of me. I tucked everything surrounding this moment away into a deep recess in my heart, storing it until I was ready to explore or explain it.

At the time, I would describe my faith as a given. I had chosen my Presbyterian husband not on the basis of his religion but for the goodness of his heart. Judge recently had seen my faith serve as an anchor through some rough waters. Breast cancer

A boy "with an old soul" and his family. Back Row: Max, Jennie, Joseph;
Front Row: Lillian, Harold, Florence.

The Rosenn family. Back Row: Lillian, Jennie, Max;
Front Row: Florence, Joseph, Harold.

U.S. Army First Lieutenant Max Rosenn served in the South Pacific during WWII.

*Max says goodbye to Tillie and young sons Keith and Daniel
as he leaves to serve his country at war.*

Grandpa Max enjoying his first granddaughter, Eva.

Signed clerkship photo: "To Mollie. With highest esteem and affection. Max Rosenn."

*Signed clerkship photo: "To Mollie. With esteem and adoration.
Max and Tillie Rosenn."*

Mollie and Judge during one of her frequent visits "home" to Pennsylvania.

Judge enjoying a walk in his community, Franklin Street, Wilkes-Barre.

Judge at age 95, reflecting in his twilight years.

Monte, Mollie, Nate, Alaina, and Erin visiting Judge in chambers during the summer of 2001.

Mollie and family visiting "first clerk" Joe Savitz and Judge's brother Harold at Rosenn, Jenkins & Greenwald in 2009.

Mollie and family visiting Joe and Janice Savitz at their Kingston, PA home in 2011.

Mollie and family enjoying a rose garden visit at Harold, Sallyanne, and Scott Rosenn's home in the summer of 2011.

had claimed yet another one of my mom's sisters, just as it had taken her life years before. And my little three-year-old niece had recently lost her battle with brain cancer.

If I had Judge back for one day, this is a moment in time I would choose to explore further with him. What did he see in me that caused him to make such a casual observation about the depth of my faith? A depth that I had not yet consciously embraced.

Learning about the development of my mentor's own faith life shed some light on his question. From an early age, he knew that he was a Jew and he took his prayer life seriously. Most of his teaching was done by wandering teachers who came to his house and taught for an hour in exchange for a meal. He was interested in Hebrew and took it upon himself to learn it.

By the time he was twelve, Max read long night prayers to his brother and sisters as he put them to bed. He grew proficient at daily services, and neighbors frequently drafted him as the tenth member of the minyan in their home. He attended Saturday Sabbath services alone while his parents worked and his siblings were too young to attend.

After his bar mitzvah, he seriously considered becoming a rabbi. His mentor was the first American-born, college-educated rabbi in the community. This Shakespearean and Latin scholar was different than any man Max had ever known. Even though the rabbi had extensive duties looking after the religious life of all six synagogues in the community, he took time to play ball with Max along the river at Kirby Park. On Friday evenings, the rabbi often dined with the local Catholic clergy, who respected his knowledge of Christian history.

Jennie could see the high regard her son had for his mentor. She also observed how the worshipers often found fault with him for not keeping up with all of his synagogue commitments. She felt that it was a position that did not enjoy the honor it deserved, and actively discouraged her son from becoming a rabbi.

Although my mentor decided not to pursue the religious life, he maintained a deep interest in it. He became a student of history and comparative religion, with a particular interest in the Protestant religions growing out of the Reformation. Each time, he came away from his studies feeling a confidence and a joy in the religious and spiritual concepts of Judaism. Through the end of his life, he delighted in performing weddings and participating in other religious celebrations.

During his college years, he discovered that the great respect he held for his Jewish culture and religion was the exception rather than the rule. His fellow Jewish students at Cornell University had little knowledge of their history or heritage. Many also lacked self-esteem, considering themselves socially inferior to their Christian classmates. Even though one-seventh of the student population at Cornell was Jewish, there was no place to worship and little formal support.

His college experience led Judge later in life to establish the Institute for Advanced Jewish Studies in Wilkes-Barre. He was motivated to develop a program for high school students to equip them for the anti-Semitism they might encounter on a college campus. He wanted to share the history of their people and to help them develop pride and a healthy self-esteem that embraced their heritage and religion.

Knowing that Judge regularly attended various synagogues and was an avid supporter of organized religion had an impact on my own faith life. He believed that practicing religion as a community brought stability and encouraged others to join and observe. He viewed his attendance as supporting both the existence of the congregations and the continuity of Jewish life. Watching him taught me that the practice of religion could be a form of respect for your religion, for your community, and for yourself.

The question Judge asked me that evening, more than any other asked in all my years of knowing him, represents to me the power of a mentor. It is the power to see things that your student cannot yet see. The power to mingle personal observations with intuition to ask a reflective question that inspires the student to explore and revisit over time. The power to gently make another aware of a new garden that he can choose to tend and grow, or not. The power to observe a part of another carved so deeply into her soul that the echoes of your words remain with her long after you are gone from her life.

With years of retrospect, I don't believe that Judge was asking me that evening if I had thought about fully embracing the religious practices of my Catholic faith. He was asking me about my heart, the precious container that holds who and what I truly love. He was asking about how I was going to express myself in this world. It was a question of authenticity and an invitation to explore my greatest truths and innermost motives.

Over the years, I've responded to his simple invitation to explore why I practice my faith, and how I will consciously choose to show up in this world as a witness to it. It was largely my mentor who inspired the courage in me to forge my own answer. And this answer suggests a glimpse of what he saw long before I embraced it from within.

Like my mentor, I chose a spiritual path that rests on a deep understanding of my religion and a respect for how others practice the religion they hold dear. Most importantly, my faith responds that others shall not know the depths of my religion simply by where they may find me on the Sabbath, but by my charity toward humanity.

> Your truest spiritual path will lead you to yourself for it is devoted to becoming.

Life's Regrets

Tears welled in Daniel's eyes as he recalled a letter he wrote after receiving a belated birthday gift from his father. "When your father is ninety-six, you have so many memories they tend to blend into an overlapping haze. After his death, I was sorting through my folder of letters and cards Dad and I had exchanged over the decades, and I came across a letter I had written to him several years ago.

"It is an oddly formal and embarrassingly pedantic letter," Daniel confessed. "Formality and intellectuality were for better or for worse a defining part of our relationship. The note is dated December 2, 1999, and it reads as follows:

Dear Dad,

I just wanted to drop you a note of thanks for the terrific book that came today marked "very Belated Birthday Gift." My only objection to this marking is that the gift is not that very late, and I actually had the vague recollection that you had already given me my birthday gift in September.

In fact, I strongly feel that you have already given me more than the full collection of gifts that a son could wish for, including the gift of life, the model of a productive and caring grown-up to try to emulate, the instillation of an ideal of responsibility to family and community, a standard of excellence to aim for in my career, and a commitment to a spiritual life.

You know that I will forever be grateful to you and Mom for all that you have given me and to my own family through the years, and that these gifts are knitted into my being.

I look forward to getting together soon.

Love,

Dan

We all have a greatest regret in life. Some acknowledge it. Some try to run from it. My mentor took it head-on. He shared the same regret with me that he had told my law professor, who had clerked twenty years before me. He wished he had been a better father to his sons and devoted more time and attention to them.

Judge explained that he lacked a role model for demonstrating love and affection. "My father, although he loved his family, seldom showed it. I suspect that he saw no model in his own home. I really didn't know what needed to be done to demonstrate love for my children. Affection is generally shown by touching and caressing, and to me that was a sign of weakness. I'm sure my father saw it the same way. It was a long time after my children had grown that I realized what I should have done to show my love and the joy it might have given me. If I could go back and live my life again, I would have displayed more visible affection for my kids, and probably for my wife, whom I loved dearly."

Although Joe Rosenn had passed long before I met Judge, I came to know him through his son's stories and the man he had become. His father's personality and background were in great contrast with those of his mother. His father was impulsive and hurried while his mother was deliberative and contemplative. His father was vigorous and daring while his mother was careful and conservative. His father was not interested in formal education while his mother carefully planned for each child's future.

Joe was a passionate and gifted athlete. He enjoyed going to New York City with his friends to watch baseball and boxing matches. He was outgoing, often to the point of being stubborn and brash. He was a man who worked hard and played harder. From his father, my mentor borrowed his energy, robustness for life, and vigor.

While Judge was overseas during World War II, his father sustained a life-altering injury. He was sparring with another man and something went terribly wrong. He spent the last twenty-five years of his life as a paraplegic. This placed an enormous burden on his family. And it made his already responsible son even more careful in predicting the consequences of his actions.

Though he grew up without a model of a loving father, Judge came to realize the importance of devoting time to his children and showing them affection. By the time I entered his life, he'd spent years setting things right with his sons. I witnessed him embracing the joys of being a grandfather and great-grandfather. His youngest son sent him off by sharing a letter thanking him for being all he could have hoped for in a father.

Watching my mentor continue to evolve until the day he died, I learned that our lives gain strength when we examine our regrets and take action to rectify them to become more of the person we seek to be. It is the small turns in life, over time, that create a vastly different future.

Life brings before us an infinite array of invitations to grow into more. We may learn what to do. We may learn how we do not want to treat others. A wise person welcomes both of these teachers.

Lineage, personality, and environment may shape you, but they do not define your full potential.

Walking with Justice

"In my travels between Amherst, Stanford, and Harvard, I have personally known or worked with four Nobel Laureates and many other distinguished and honored professors and physicians. Yet I have no hesitation in saying that I respect and admire my father over any other person I have ever known.

"In a world of increasing dishonesty and deceit, he practiced an old-time, small-town morality of basic decency, fairness, courtliness, and modesty. He was a good man, which, as someone once said, when all is said and done, it's the finest anyone could say of any man.

"Leaving all the tributes and the praise aside, my father was indeed a very good man."

My mentor's mission statement as a federal jurist was this simple: Be a good judge.

He made a commitment the day he was sworn in. "When I was elevated to the bench, I not only swore to uphold the Constitution but also *resolved* to be a good judge. I had no aspiration to be a great scholar or to achieve special distinction. I just wanted to be a good judge." He had the wisdom to understand that it was in being a good man that he would fulfill this commitment.

In his eyes, justice went beyond the law and legal precedence. He saw values as the cornerstone of adjudicating the behavior of people, and he believed those instilled in him as a young boy would serve him well. These values included morality, honesty, fairness, a respect for the dignity of the individual, and the absence of hatred or bigotry. They rested on a deep patriotism and respect for our country and its laws. They were housed in humility and a strong work ethic.

A good judge does not cease his duties when he closes the door to his chambers. My mentor committed to a high level of responsibility for living a life of moderation and discipline, and he modeled his ethics as a teacher. He never sat me down and said, "You need to do this and this and this." He showed me broad life principles through his choices and behavior. The same principles that made me a better lawyer also made me a better wife and mom and teacher and person.

This principle-based living is what defined Judge as a *servant mentor*. A mentor shares shortcuts and encourages students to use better methods to produce better results. A servant mentor starts with principles. Living these principles drives the process and methods used to make a bigger impact. A mentor leaves you inspired, wanting to *do* more and believing that you can. A servant mentor inspires you to *become* more, devoted to serving others and believing that there is no other way to live. From inside out, a servant mentor leaves an indelible thumbprint on the soul of another.

My mentor viewed with remorse the lack of integrity that was becoming more and more common in corporate and political life as we entered the twenty-first century. He believed too many of our politicians were more concerned about retaining their public office than serving the people they were elected to serve. Too many corporate executives were more concerned with their own compensation than the duty owed to their shareholders and to the public.

He surmised: "History tells us that the fall of the Holy Roman Empire occurred not because of the external attacks by the Visigoths or the peoples who surrounded them, but by the moral decay—particularly in the commercial life of the countries that formed the Roman Empire. This should be a warning to us.

These corporations owe a commitment to their shareholders, to a consuming public, and to this country."

Judge was a strong proponent of lifelong character development education, recognizing the universal principles that have endured through the ages and served as the moral foundation of our country. "These basic principles include the sanctity of life, the validity of truth, the primacy of justice. These are fundamental principles in living. They need to be taught not only at home but also in our schools and colleges and business schools. They need to be part of the spiritual life of the community, whether you belong to a church, a synagogue, or a mosque. A sense of ethics and integrity needs to be taught and repeated time after time."

My mentor piqued and nurtured my interest in business ethics, a topic I speak about today. He also lit a fire in me to work with our youth. He advised me to teach my children and students well and to remind myself of these ethical guidelines often. Through his eyes, the future of mankind rests on these principles of living.

In the Bible, the most common pairing of words is "justice" and "righteousness," based on the idea that God imparts to rulers a sense of justice, and this helps them judge all their people fairly. This pairing guided my mentor's every decision. It was his passionate pursuit of justice that enabled him to adjudicate with righteousness, be a dutiful and generous steward of all he had been given, and seize opportunities to honor the dignity within each human.

Max Rosenn was indeed a very good man.

Freedom flourishes upon
the bedrock of ethics and integrity.

Humility and Honor

Daniel took his seat as his brother, Keith, a professor of law at the University of Miami, stood and walked to the front of the synagogue. Just as his younger brother had done, Keith began by thanking his father's community for their support and attendance. He gave a special thank-you to the doctors who had supported his dad through his final illness.

"Dad was fortunate to have been so often eulogized during his lifetime. A few months ago, I, like many in this synagogue, sat in Wilkes University and watched a marvelous film celebrating my father's life. Tributes to him appear in the pages of the Federal Reporter, *in newspapers and magazines. A more concrete memorial sits around the corner as the Max Rosenn Federal Courthouse."*

Long after my clerkship ended, friends in Wilkes-Barre sent me press clippings so I could keep up with the local news. One of my favorite headlines arrived when the federal government renamed the building where Judge went to work each day in his honor. On the day this news broke, it read, "Rosenn Name Perfectly Suits Courthouse: It Reflects Justice and Service."

As his clerk, I regularly attended award ceremonies recognizing my mentor's contributions. It was as if he had a rare opportunity to hear, in advance, what would be said at his funeral. Just as eulogies tend to focus on how the deceased treated others rather than what they achieved, these celebrations went beyond some poor soul attempting an abbreviated litany of Judge's years of public service in all branches of state and federal government.

I saw my mentor toasted by colleagues, former clerks, attorneys, and politicians as a man who earned admiration, respect, and trust. They explored his immense understanding of humanity that sprang from a life of community involvement. They marveled at his consuming interest in the world around him.

When the local bar association renamed its library the Max Rosenn Memorial Library, the speaker, Attorney Joseph Cosgrove, used the opportunity to celebrate a patriot. "When his country was in peril and at war and he was asked to serve, he said yes. When his commonwealth needed his services as a lawyer to help bring relief to those most afflicted, he was asked to serve, and he said yes. And when the president of the United States and the Senate asked him to serve as a judge, he said yes.

"Each time, he responded as a servant, and a profound servant he always was, because he had one love among many that guided his life, and that was love of the law and a friendship with the Constitution. In preserving that Constitution, expanding its protections and its liberties, he is among the most celebrated of patriots."

Attorney Cosgrove explained why naming the library after Judge was such a befitting honor. "Every day there's something new in that library. There's a new case, a statute, an article, a discussion, a criticism, an argument. There's life in that library. And so, what began in the Anglo-American system eight hundred years ago as a conversation about how civilized people were to live with one another continues. And in our midst there has never been a more important, a more humble, a more respected voice than that of Judge Rosenn. His voice will continue to resound in these halls and in that library as lawyers of the future, who did not have the opportunity to know him, enter this structure in his honor. They will engage in that same conversation. Hopefully, they will hear an echo or they will see that sometimes wry little smile, and they will be as inspired as we have been by having been touched by so great a person."

As eloquent as each living eulogy was, it was the experience of watching Judge respond to them that is deeply seared into my being. The achievements for which my mentor was recognized put him in an elite category of statesmanship. Yet, it seemed the more he was honored, the more his servant's heart shone through.

He turned his attention fully to those who gathered to honor him. He spoke like a poet, without a note, sharing stunning impromptu verses of grace and heartfelt gratitude. One by one, he edified each person who spoke in his tribute, telling stories of their shared pasts and bringing the audience to laughter. He thanked by name those who he knew had a hand in organizing the event as well as those invisible persons who assisted.

He acknowledged that we're all influenced and shaped by circumstances and people who affect our destiny. He paid tribute to his family and all of those who contributed to his accomplishments. He generously shared credit with his law clerks and secretary. He noted how much he cherished his friendship with his past clerks and expressed pride that many had gone on to distinguished service in the legal, educational, and public service fields.

It struck me that he never said he was *humbled*. He often said he was honored.

Judge taught me that humility does not mean thinking less of yourself in any way; it means not thinking about yourself at all. It flows not from your ego but from your heartfelt gratitude for the gifts you've been given and the opportunity to use them in the service of others. True humility is not about bringing yourself down. It is about reflecting back to others how they have enlarged you.

Many of the specific words spoken have evaporated over time, yet the emotions wrapped around his message, delivered from his heart to each person in the audience, I carry with me to this day. His elegance and wisdom stirred my soul. His humorous quips delighted it. His humility inspired it.

A humble spirit stands as a mirror, reflecting the brilliance shining from within others and magnifying all gifts back to the giver.

From the first day I met him, Judge subtly communicated the promise he saw shining from within me. Despite my inexperience, he made me feel good about myself as a lawyer and as a person. He rewarded my efforts with kind words. When I tripped and wanted to look at my failure, he uplifted me with encouragement and reconnected me to the greatness he knew I carried within. He set a strong expectation that as I learned a better way, I would do better. This constant reflection of his belief in my personal excellence inspired me to become more for myself, for my community, and for mankind.

Judge was a mirror. And nowhere was this more obvious than when people gathered, oftentimes standing room only, to honor him.

> Let others see their own greatness
> when looking in your eyes.

The Storyteller

Keith lightened his tone in an attempt to uplift the crowd. "Dad was a model of virtue and had few vices. The only laws I ever saw him take liberty with were the speed limits. But that was genetic.

"One of his first cases was the defense of his father, Grandpa Joe, when the authorities sought to lift his license for excessive speeding violations. When he found out my grandfather had been convicted of speeding twelve times that month, he said, 'Go ahead, take away his license. He's a public nuisance.'"

The crowd laughed. Keith added, "My grandfather always maintained that my father was a lousy lawyer because of that case."

My evidence professor taught that the most successful trial lawyers create a story for juries. They paint a vivid picture and draw the jurors into the story line. People resonate with stories because we're wired to listen to and retell our oral history. For generations, our history has been passed down by story. I remember thinking how much sense this made. After all, Jesus himself taught in parables. And what are parables but stories?

It was not until I studied at the side of Judge that I came to fully appreciate the power of a good story. As a lawyer, mentor, and legal scholar, he used stories to connect with others, explain his view of the world, and inspire others to action.

I spent hours listening to him share details of his life and tales of youthful escapades. Some of my favorite stories came from a 1928 road trip he and a friend took from New York to California, mostly on dirt roads, in a little two-seater Chevrolet. They drove the northern route out and the southern route back, visiting several national parks and seeing sculptors carve Mount Rushmore into the stone of the Black Hills. His stories never got old—even when he repeated some of them—because of his enjoyment in the telling. His eyes lit up with genuine delight as he laughed along with his listeners.

The story of his father, the renegade driver, was another favorite. Judge told how his father played down the matter, very casually saying to him, "I have a hearing at the courthouse for the revocation of my license and I'd like you to represent me." He said he'd be glad to do it. Upon walking into the courthouse, he met an old friend, who was the examiner for the State of Pennsylvania. The examiner asked if he had seen his father's file. He had not.

When Max looked at the file, his face blanched. His father had never told him that he had been arrested a dozen times for speeding. Now he was being cited for the revocation of his license.

This was serious because his father needed the car for business. Max asked him, "Why didn't you tell me this? How can you drive around the country with twelve fines?"

His father became indignant. "Do you realize I drive fifty thousand miles a year buying cattle and I could not cover this much ground unless I travel quickly? I have to move quickly."

"Well, you're going to have to move quickly and get another lawyer," Max retorted, "because I'm not going to represent you in this case. You deserve to lose your license." The young lawyer walked out of the courtroom, leaving his father standing there. Joe Rosenn lost his license for three months. He didn't talk to his son for even longer.

My mentor told this story in a way that left listeners in

stitches, while clearly delivering his message: you must hold on to ethics and standards of justice, no matter the pressure or client.

=====

Sometimes Judge threw his students into a more active role in learning the power of a good story. His first law clerk, Joe Savitz, experienced such a lesson as a young, green lawyer.

Joe had recently joined Rosenn, Jenkins & Greenwald when Max had a beautiful tree in front of his home killed by a leak from a gas line. He tried to work out a settlement with the owner of the gas company but found him to be a disagreeable and unreasonable man.

Without hesitation, Max turned to the court system. He trusted the system for resolving disputes that needed the help of the law. Long before he was an appellate court judge, he believed that if the lower court failed in delivering justice, parties should appeal to a higher court that brought greater legal acuity and experience.

He came into Joe's office one day. "Come with me, we're going to court."

"What for?"

"I'll tell you on the way."

On the stroll to the courthouse, Max said: "I have a case coming up, and I want you to be my lawyer. I am suing a gas company for killing my tree."

"When's the case?"

"Right now."

As an inexperienced lawyer, Joe was completely unprepared to appear before the court on such a matter. He protested, "But I haven't done any research on the value of the tree!"

"You don't have to," Max said. "You just need to ask me three questions, and I'll handle the rest."

"Three questions? What are the three questions?"

"My name, my address, and 'Can you tell the court why you are here?'"

When it was time to go before the judge, Max was sworn in. His student did as instructed. "For the record sir, what is your name?"

"Max Rosenn."

"And your address?"

"100 Third Avenue, Kingston, Pennsylvania."

With two questions down, Joe took a deep breath and asked, "Now, can you tell the court why you are here?"

Max responded, throwing himself into the story of his loss. He talked for fifteen minutes about his glorious tree, sharing detail after detail. With eloquent description, he described its girth. He informed the court how the number of rings reflected the age. He spoke of its beauty and the important role it played in his life. He told the court how the gas company's actions took the life of his tree. He quantified its value. He left nothing out.

Green as Joe was, when his boss finished his story of love and loss, he knew he had one final thing to contribute. "Your honor, Plaintiff rests."

The gas company's attorney could not make any headway on cross-examination. He rested. The judge's verdict came quickly: Ruling in favor of the plaintiff.

From the dinner table to his chambers to a court of law, Judge used stories to connect with, teach, and inspire his students. Law is a technical field and can be a dry subject matter. He brought it to life for his students through story. He evoked our emotions and our imagination. His stories engaged us and helped us frame up our world in a new way.

Judge's stories had a theme. They taught lessons and uplifted others. Most of them were entertaining. And those that highlighted the worst of humanity allowed listeners to be fully present with pain and loss because he artfully weaved in strands of resiliency, regeneration, and hope.

My mentor knew the secret known by poets and writers and singers. Stories are the language of the heart. They elicit action and transformation in a way that facts never will.

> Behind a life of influence you will find a masterful storyteller.

A Patriot's Heart

"Dad was appointed as a judge of the United States Court of Appeals for the Third Circuit when he was sixty years old and a very successful lawyer. Serving as a judge was a position for which he was eminently suited.

"He brought to the bench a wealth of trial experience and practical lawyering skills. He had been both prosecutor and defense counsel, a lawyer for savings and loans and commercial banks, and a high-powered labor lawyer. He managed to represent both management and labor unions, something few labor lawyers have accomplished.

"He also brought a wealth of public service. He served eighteen months in the Philippines as a JAG lieutenant in the U.S. Army

during World War II. He went on to serve as Pennsylvania Secretary of Public Welfare under two governors."

Judge dedicated his life to serving his beloved country. One of the most significant callings he felt was in the early 1940s as the Germans marched across Europe taking over other countries. By that time, France had been occupied and the French Vichy government was collaborating with the Nazis. Belgium, Poland, and other countries had become a victim of Germany. England was in grave danger of being defeated. From Judge's perspective, the structure of Western civilization and everything that the Allies stood for was at stake. There was a need for more men.

As a thirty-five-year-old married father of two young sons and a part-time public defender, he was exempt from the draft. Despite these valid exemptions and a growing law practice, he felt a moral duty to take an active part in the war.

He attempted to enlist in the navy but was repeatedly declined because of high blood pressure, which checked out normal by his physician back home. After further investigation, he discovered that neither the Philadelphia nor the Washington recruiting office was accepting Jewish officers. He gave up on the navy, repackaged himself as a gifted mechanic, and entered the army. After fighting his way into the war, he shipped out to the Philippines.

As difficult as it was to leave his family, Max felt he was doing the right thing. "If it called for a sacrifice of life, that was a price that would have to be paid. The cause was important for the preservation of civilization and for the preservation of the United States. I believed that my wife would get along with our sons the best she could. I was prepared to make almost any sacrifice to serve and contribute to a victory. A love for my country, for me, is almost to the effect as the love for immediate family."

The question to his patriotic heart was not why he would serve, but how could he not. He recalled, "I felt elated when I got into the army because I was able to make a contribution to a cause that affected so many. I felt like I had something to offer to fulfill my commitment to myself and my government." He had been elated, joyful. This was the same spirit of service I witnessed fifty years later.

Max's foresight and wise investments helped alleviate the burden on his wife and children, who would have struggled greatly to live on the little money he earned as a military man. During the housing decline of the Great Depression, he had bought a low-priced four-family apartment house. This investment not only produced income, but also kept Tillie occupied during the war period.

He further eased his absence by visiting a garden adjacent to the military headquarters. With each letter home, he picked a beautiful, pungent gardenia and folded it into the envelope. The flower retained its fragrance across the ocean. To Tillie, it smelled like love.

My mentor often recalled the greatest lesson he had learned at war: men should not be judged by their uniform or by superficial appearances, but by their character. He explained, "I discovered very quickly that a man might be a colonel in an army but not have any more character than a private. In times of great need and stress, I found more times I could rely on the private for support and help than I could on the colonel. The *individual* is the determining factor in making judgments rather than making them on superficial appearances of people or their uniforms. You don't have to wear beautiful clothes or formal clothes to have dignity, honesty, truthfulness, and integrity."

Upon his return from the war, he carried this lesson into his work in state government. Snippets of Judge's executive branch service came out through his stories, yet I was surprised when I learned the full impact of his service.

In 1966, the year I was born, he was appointed to run the

second-largest department of public health in the country with an annual budget of a half billion dollars. Under his leadership, Pennsylvania streamlined services while expanding benefits and creating thousands of jobs.

His passion for education and compassion for others superseded his relatively conservative personal lifestyle as he sought to fully understand people different from him. He quickly became known for running the department in the most nonpartisan, nonpolitical way it had ever experienced.

Intimate exposure to the insidious nature of prejudice and the caustic effects of discrimination impacted him deeply. In a time of great social tensions, he became a champion for those who needed governmental assistance, including children, the elderly, the poor, minorities, and those with disabilities. His commission desegregated public schools. It promoted landmark legislation to open up education, housing, and employment to all.

He developed the Head Start Program for early childhood education in his state. It was so successful that the federal government used it as the model for a national rollout of the program.

He saw as inhumane the mandatory institutionalization of the mentally ill. He led Pennsylvania to become the first state in the nation to distinguish mental retardation as a disability from mental illness as a disease.

Of all of his accomplishments, he was most proud of providing opportunities to people to attend schools, live in neighborhoods, and work jobs that had never before been open to them.

The *individual* is the determining factor in making judgments rather than making them on superficial appearances; he had learned this lesson well. His execution of this truth brought his state and this country closer to its ideal of forming a more perfect union.

> Your value lies not in status or title,
> but in the roots of your character
> and depth of your compassion.

Military and Civility

"Dad came to the bench with few preconceptions. He was the antithesis of an ideologue. He had a very strong sense of what was right, fair, and just. He abhorred racial and religious bigotry and intolerance."

Keith joked, "If you're going to have a bias, that's a pretty good bias to have."

"He worked within the confines of the Constitution and the law, the facts set forth in the record, and the arguments of counsel. He had great respect for other lawyers and a well-deserved reputation for treating counsel arguing before him fairly and civilly."

Everywhere Max looked in the Philippines, he saw waste. As American military units were evacuated, they left behind their trucks and equipment. Some were bulldozed over cliffs when the men moved out. Countless craft carriers and boats sat in rivers and along the ocean shoreline.

Max also saw potential. Filipino civilians expressed interest in purchasing the sunken watercraft. These fine craftsmen were capable of fixing the motors and quickly rebuilding the boats. Enterprising entrepreneurs, mostly Chinese, gathered the thousands of empty oil drums abandoned in fields or near landing strips to resell them.

Max reported the abandoned equipment to his headquarters in Manila. He recommended that they adopt a policy of selling abandoned equipment "as is" to settle claims that people had against the United States. This exchange would not only help his country but also provide Filipino civilians the means to move from city to city and island to island.

Despite several follow-up letters, Max heard nothing back. He really wasn't surprised, given that it seemed few in the army did any more than they had to. Frustrated, he decided to adopt a course of action of his own. As a licensed commissioner of claims, he had the authority to investigate and decide claims. He posted notices on trees and in the cities directed to anyone who had a legitimate claim against the United States. He described the equipment that would be sold, the date of sale, and the "as is" condition.

Qualified bidders could purchase equipment up to the amount of their claim. He structured the sale this way because he didn't want to handle money or run the risk of someone accusing him of not turning over the proceeds.

His sale of submerged boats and other equipment generated millions of dollars. He decided the claims and gave the United States credit for the purchase price of each item. He then sent a report to headquarters detailing the claims.

The next day he received a message: report immediately to Colonel Wood by the first available military aircraft to Manila headquarters. He knew he was going to be taken to task, possibly facing a court-martial. He instructed his officers, "If I don't come back, send my gear home."

A major greeted him upon arrival in Manila. "Oh, you're in big trouble." He shepherded Max in to see Colonel Wood, the chief of claims operation in the South Pacific. The colonel was furious. Waving Max's report in the air, he shouted, "Where did you get the authority to do this?"

"Colonel, I got tired of sticking my head in the sand and decided to stick it out. I thought the sales were worthwhile and desirable. You may remember I sent you a report of what was going on. I felt that it was important for us to save our government millions of dollars and at the same time provide very necessary transportation for the civilians."

"*Where* did you get the authority?" the colonel repeated.

"The commanding general in the field has the authority to dispose of abandoned property."

"Since when are you the commanding general in the field?"

"I'm not, but I have the authority. Before I started out on this course, I checked the regulations and was in touch with the commanding general in the field. I not only had his authority but also his blessing. In some instances, we needed gasoline to move the equipment, and he saw that I got gasoline for that purpose."

"And where did you get the authority to communicate with the commanding general in the field?"

Max was prepared for the question. "I was seven hundred fifty miles from headquarters, separated by islands and ocean. You were advised, but I never got a reply. Therefore, my only alternative was to communicate with the commanding general in the field."

In a calmer voice, Colonel Wood asked, "Can you type?"

"Yes, I can type."

"Well, you are going to stay here and give me a detailed report of abandoned property, with your recommendations." Max gathered his notes. Over the next two days, he typed up his recommendations and completed the report.

One week after returning to his base, an order came through from General Styers, the commander in chief of the U.S. Army Forces in the Western Pacific, adopting Max's recommendations as the new policy for the disposal of abandoned property.

Only later, when he spent a few days at headquarters on his way home to Pennsylvania, would he learn that General Styers decorated Colonel Wood for formulating the new policy.

There he found a copy of his report with two changes. The first page, which he had directed to Colonel Wood, had been retyped and directed to General Styers. The last page, which he had signed with his recommendations, was now signed by Colonel Wood.

Max walked away with the satisfaction that the Filipinos were beneficiaries of the new policy and that the Americans were a few million dollars ahead.

He also walked away with a new understanding of how terrible it feels to not be credited for your work. He made a promise to always do his best to be fair and generous with credit and praise for others.

Who would have guessed that one man's selfishness would

trigger in another man a great talent for affirming others and making them feel good about their work and themselves? Thank you, Colonel Wood, for teaching my mentor this lesson. It changed my life.

> Each life experience whispers
> this question:
> How do you want to be changed
> because of me?

Destiny Calls

"Despite his illustrious career in government, it was my father's devotion to law that most defined his life. After graduating from the University of Pennsylvania Law School in 1932, no job at a large law firm awaited him. He had to struggle to establish a law practice in the heart of the Great Depression. He went on to become a principal partner in one of the area's premier law firms.

"Accepting a judicial appointment meant taking a substantial cut in income. I never once heard him complain.

"He never expressed any regrets about having become a judge. It was a position he clearly loved."

Max returned home from the war with a grand vision. His respect for the law had only grown stronger while he was away serving his country. To him, practicing law was not only a business but also a profession with the power to make a meaningful contribution to the world.

He envisioned bringing together legal specialists to better serve clients. This would require him to move beyond his partnership with his brother Harold to found a new law firm. The firm of Rosenn, Jenkins & Greenwald would become the largest law firm in northeast Pennsylvania.

From its inception, Max embedded processes to serve clients with a culture of compassion. He paired this with an emphasis on efficiency and ingenuity. He sought to instill in all those around him that a progressive culture is not defined simply by innovation and technology, but by kindness and care.

He structured the firm with the secretaries sitting in the reception area, answering the phones for the multiple partners. In this time before office copy machines, each legal filing required the secretaries to type through eight copies of carbon paper, needing to correct each mistake by hand eight times. When Max heard of a machine that would relieve the secretaries from sitting and taking notes by hand, he welcomed the use of this new technology to streamline the work. He was the first attorney in town to purchase a dictating machine. The secretaries played back recordings on a RCA Victrola with a large horn.

One of the greatest challenges to his desired culture of compassion was a secretary named Louisa. She was described by one of the firm partners as a good egg, but well scrambled. This woman with a strong English accent had developed a habit of speaking loudly because she primarily served attorney Greenwald who had lost much of his hearing from cancer. Her voice echoed down the halls.

To make matters worse, Louisa made no secret that she fostered a great dislike for answering phones. She tended to treat callers as inconveniences and let them know they were interrupting her valuable work. One day in October 1970, the phone rang, disturbing Louisa. Others in the firm listened to her taking a message with a great deal of irritation in her voice.

"What's your name? Nixon. How do you spell it?"

"What's your first name? Richard?"

"No, attorney Rosenn is too busy to talk right now."

"When? He'll call you back when he has time, that's when. He's a busy man."

Click.

A while later, Max stopped by to pick up his messages. "Louisa, when did you get this message?"

"About an hour ago."

"Do you know who this is?"

"Some guy named Richard Nixon."

The loud English woman who did not know American politics had rudely dismissed a call from none other than the president of the United States!

Although Max would soon instruct Louisa about his expectations for professionally answering the telephone, this was not his most immediate task. He went to his office and promptly returned the call. A call that started the process of him becoming the Honorable Max Rosenn, esteemed federal judge of the United States Third Circuit Court of Appeals.

Destiny had called, and although the secretary did not seem to care, its name was spelled N-i-x-o-n.

> Listen for the call of your destiny,
> and when it comes,
> release your plans and follow.

Justice for All

As a fellow lawyer, Keith held a deep appreciation of his father's impact on the legal community. "Virtually no one other than Dad continued to turn out high-quality appellate opinions at the ripe old age of ninety-six. Our research librarian at the University of Miami once set out to find out the exact number of opinions Dad authored. She gave up after seven hundred opinions.

"She also set out to find how often his opinions had been cited, and abandoned that quest after researching just forty of his opinions. Why? Those opinions had been cited more than thirty-six hundred times by other judges.

"A few years ago I read a piece that claimed Dad was the fifth most cited federal court of appeals judge."

An appellate court judgeship is a scholar's job. Writing opinions subject to review by the Supreme Court of the United States and setting precedent for other judicial bodies addressing America's most demanding and complex issues carries a flavor of academia. Pairing this intellectual pursuit with a deep sense of humanity is rarely reflected in judicial opinions. This is what set apart my mentor.

Watching Judge draft an opinion at the law library table surrounded by documents and stacks of books left no doubt as to his fidelity to the law. Learning how he drew upon his immense humanity and practical wisdom to explore from every side the concerns of the parties whose lives his decision might affect was life changing.

His unyielding pursuit of the truth came through as he recounted cases, asking out loud the questions he undoubtedly asked as he decided the cases. "*How* can you run a company with this condition in place?" or "*What* are the *options* for a woman who is mixed up with a drug dealer and trying to support her children?"

Each case brought an invitation to pursue the truth with pure motives. "Truth when spoken with bad intent beats all the lies that you can invent," Judge said, quoting nineteenth-century poet William Blake. "If this is possible of truth, depending on the motivation," he reflected, "just think what happens when a half truth or partial truth is conveyed."

In the throes of discussing his impassioned disagreement with a colleague's position on a case, he was known to strike his fist on the library table and exclaim, "Justice, justice, justice!" Although his empathy for a party might not bring a ruling in its favor, it helped ensure justice. His participation in a case brought a guarantee that the decision makers would seek to fully understand all of the circumstances before judging.

As a practicing attorney, my mentor once said to the judge he was appearing before, "You are using the law to subvert the law." The court went on to use this phrase in its opinion, and it has been repeated by lawyers and judges throughout the country many times over.

Nowhere was Judge's abiding concern over compromising justice more apparent than in his review of cases subject to the Federal Sentencing Guidelines. These guidelines were intended to provide uniformity in sentencing. He was concerned that they disempowered judges as decision makers and resulted in lengthy mandatory sentences. He didn't believe that just because two people committed a drug crime that they should have the same sentence imposed on them.

Sitting in my office discussing my first sentencing case, Judge explained, "To the extent the guidelines avoid disparities, they often do so at the cost of undermining just punishment. They've led to our country issuing sentences ten to fifteen times longer than any other nation in the world for comparable crime. It hasn't been shown that these long sentences deter crime. As an enlightened nation, we can do better than this."

He did not hesitate to uphold weighty sentences when justified by the facts of the case. Yet, he wrote opinions with strong language when he felt that the guidelines were being applied in a way that disregarded important facts, unnecessarily broke up families, and required taxpayers to maintain wives and children for extraordinarily long terms.

He emphasized that it was not the appellate court, Congress, nor the Sentencing Commission that had the agonizing moral burden of sentencing a convicted defendant. This, he asserted, fell to the sentencing trial judge. He posed the question: "Can we, sitting separately and far removed from the center where punishment is meted out to flesh and blood, require that a sentencing judge impose a sentence that the judge conscientiously believes is fundamentally impractical, unsound, and unjust?"

My mentor's pursuit of justice also flared in immigration cases. While praising the government's goal of expediting the removal of criminal aliens, he recognized the heart-wrenching pain for families and burdens for employers that accompany deportation proceedings. He suggested to Congress that denying decision makers the discretion to consider the type of crime and the familial conditions of the offender could be harsh, self-defeating, and unwise.

As one of the most cited appellate court judges in the history of the United States, my mentor's work will be relied on by lawyers and judges for years to come. In reading his opinions, they will take their own walk with justice as they experience a brilliant and analytical mind tempered by a deep compassion for humanity.

Yet, you don't need to be a lawyer or to wade through legal opinions to benefit from Judge's life wisdom. As a researcher and trainer, I've come to realize over the past two decades that most people don't need me to cite study after study in order to make positive change. If an audience wants the science behind the success principles, I happily provide it. But most people simply want the tools my research suggests will help them. They hunger for the truths to which this research leads.

We are designed as humans to know truth when we hear it. When we are in a state of calm, unmoved by the noise of the world, truth resonates within us. Even when hearing a fact for the first time, we can find ourselves nodding our heads, as if we've heard it before. We have the sense of being reminded of what we already know. It simply makes sense.

Justice holds this same quality. Humans at our highest

functioning are designed to love and to treat others with compassion and fairness. This is the truth that resonates from within Judge's legal opinions and his life. For, his passion for justice echoes in practically every syllable he ever expressed.

> High above the noisy fearmongering of critics and cynics softly speaks your true self.

A Judge's Judge

"I believe Dad's work as a Court of Appeals judge provided him with his reason for living, especially in the thirteen years since Mother's death.

"He had great affection and admiration for his colleagues on the bench."

With his father's humility, Keith added, "I have every reason to believe that they had great affection and admiration for him as well."

Shortly before Judge's twenty-fifth anniversary on the bench, my co-clerk and I huddled up with his secretary, Barbara, to talk about how we could properly acknowledge the milestone.

His secretary administered the chambers with a strong hand. She was clear about how she wanted things done and let us clerks know when she felt we were stepping out of line. She was loyal to Judge, extremely protective of him, and visibly proud to serve him. Barbara's admiration for our boss prompted a brilliant idea. "Given how much his colleagues think of Judge, how about we ask them to send congratulatory notes, and then we'll make a memory book for him?"

She sent requests for a short congratulatory note to celebrate Judge's impending anniversary. Contributions came pouring in from Supreme Court justices, appellate court colleagues, district court judges, and state court judges from across the country.

I spent hours reading and compiling letters that went beyond a short note of congratulations to recall intimate details of the richness my boss had brought to the authors' lives. Colleagues who had served by his side for years noted the depth of his scholarly contributions, expressed gratitude for his commitment to the court, commended his compassion and sense of fairness, and bowed to his unfailing respect for humanity. He was honored as a judge's judge, the most honorable in a group of honorables.

Several judges, who wrote eloquent opinions as a livelihood, confessed insufficient words to describe this great servant of the public. They resorted to quoting words of ancient philosophers and poets as a tribute to his nobility and active soul.

Many judges referred to him as a Renaissance man. One eloquent note from Judge Edward Becker stated: "It is so difficult to adequately describe this remarkable human being. The best word I can summon is 'prince.' Max Rosenn is a prince—a man of quintessential grace, elegance, gentility, civility, nobility, magnanimity, unselfishness, philanthropy, decency, courtesy, tact, wisdom, and sagacity—all qualities of the princely status."

Judge Timothy Lewis, whom I'd recently met as the newest member of the Third Circuit, wrote that he was struck by Judge's genteel manner from the moment of his warm welcome in the robing room. He shared how a dinner invitation from Judge Rosenn caused him to wonder what they would talk about and ended up being one of the most interesting and entertaining evenings of his life:

> *I listened with lively interest to the reminiscence of your days with the Pennsylvania Human Relations Commission during the 1960s; the stories of your law school experiences and your early career*

as a lawyer; your personal encounters with and commitment to fighting against discrimination and inequality; and your obvious love of the law. And then, to my surprise and great pleasure, you engaged me in a discussion of world politics— spanning the imminent invasion of Haiti by U.S. troops, peace negotiations in the Middle East, and the new Russia. As I tried to keep up, I could not help thinking to myself, 'My goodness, now this is a judge: wise, worldly, sophisticated, informed, and a true gentlemen.' As we walked back to the hotel, I tried to cram as many questions into the two-block stretch as I possibly could. I knew then, as I know now, that this is a man from whom I might learn, not just about the art of judging, but about the beauty of a quiet dignity.

For me as a young lawyer, it was a special thrill to hold letters from United States Supreme Court justices in my hands. These letters told how the highest jurists in the land benefited from my mentor's adept judicial skills and shared their pleasure at having such a remarkable, warm, and decent human being as a colleague.

One day a letter arrived from Samuel Alito, who would go on to sit on the Supreme Court. He recalled how Judge had instilled in him a sense of dedication when, as a young law clerk, Alito first met the man:

> *I remember meeting you for the first time shortly after I began my clerkship with Leonard Garth. My impression of you then is almost identical to my impression of you now: dignified, courteous, and warm (even to a lowly law clerk), and extremely well prepared and incisive on the bench. Looking back, I find it both remarkable and impressive that the Judge Max Rosenn I have known as a law clerk, as an attorney, and as a judicial colleague is almost exactly the same. Neither the passage of time nor the changes in my position have altered my perception of you. Throughout, my image of you has remained that of a dedicated, learned, courteous, and fair jurist: the very epitome of what a judge should be.*

This rocklike stability over time explains why I have a photo of Judge sitting on my office desk. At the end of my first year with him, he called me into his office and gave me this photo of him holding Tillie close as they danced at their wedding anniversary celebration. We had shared the journey of his wife's loss, and I accepted it as a prized possession. Taking out a pen, he signed, "With deepest affection and respect, Max and Tillie Rosenn."

It's the same reason I have a more formal portrait of Judge in his robes on my home office desk. This was a gift from him upon the sad day of my final departure from my clerkship. He signed it, "With highest esteem and affection, Max Rosenn."

It also explains why across the country there are judges, lawyers, deans of law schools, business professionals, and others with a photo of Judge Rosenn on their desks. He continues to watch over us, with his dignified, wise, and warm presence captured in a moment of time.

When facing tough decisions, we pause, look to him, and ask, "Judge, what would you do?" In the stillness, fueled by an integrity that withstands the passage of time, we hear his answer. Some things are not changed by the quicksands of time.

> Integrity is a powerful force, keeping you alive to others long after you've left their presence.

Quiet Leader

"Dad was not only a great judge but also someone with great dedication to public and community service. He built his own law practice, one client at a time, and he always felt a deep sense of obligation to this community that made that possible.

"Dad always told me: 'A man can never have enough friends, but one enemy is one too many.' He had friends wherever he went, and he cultivated those friendships. He also did a great deal of pro bono work and involved himself with numerous charitable, civic, educational, religious, and fraternal organizations, which he supported generously.

"When duty called, he spearheaded the effort to rebuild Wyoming Valley after the devastating flood from tropical storm Agnes in 1972."

The wrath of Agnes was drastic and swift. One billion dollars of damage in one weekend.

As the Wyoming Valley prepared to commemorate the twentieth anniversary of its disastrous flood, I got an intensive education about the catastrophic event that shaped the area. The media recounted in detail the prominent role my boss, as chair of the Flood Recovery Task Force, played in the rebuilding of his community.

Years later, I personally tasted the state of shock and disbelief when my city of Cedar Rapids experienced the devastating flood of 2008. Businesses that had led the community were wiped out. Many nonprofit organizations that had provided help to those in need were gone. Even if one's home or business wasn't personally destroyed, all were affected because the downtown and other whole areas of the city had disappeared overnight.

I could easily imagine the leaders gathering in Wilkes-Barre after the flood, asking questions. How can we rebuild? What will this look like? How soon can we start? How do we even begin to move forward?

The answers to their questions created a consensus. There was only one man who had the executive experience to coordinate the massive cleanup efforts and the vision to reinvent a modern community. There was only one man who had connections to federal, state, and regional governments and was respected by both the public and private sectors. There was only one man who knew who to talk to and how to bring the quick relief needed.

The day after the flood waters receded, community leaders slogged through the silt and debris, over garbage and discarded treasures. Toppled utility poles exposed deadly live wires. The men walked past storefronts with broken windows, beneath watermarks staining the second and third stories. Inside the deserted buildings, the sewage, electrical, and telephone systems were decimated.

They made their way down the street and knocked on the door of the old Wilkes-Barre post office, now known as the Max Rosenn Federal Courthouse. Providing fresh oxygen to the air wretched with mildew, Judge agreed to serve without hesitation. He did not step up because he wanted to be a leader. He saw there was a job to do, and he had the resources to best get it done and help those in need.

"Our community was paralyzed," explained Judge. "I knew I was in a position to help with my personal connections at the federal and state levels. I called Senator Hugh Scott and he agreed to meet me to tour the area. I was standing near him when he called President Nixon, saying, 'Mr. President, this is the greatest national disaster this country has ever had.'"

The great philosopher Lao Tzu notes that the greatest leader is the one who people barely know exists. "When his work is done, his aim fulfilled, they will say, 'We did it ourselves.'" This was the type of leader Judge was. He never sought to take credit for the accomplishments of the politicians or task force.

Members of the task force listened to him. There was no bullying or pushing. He simply motivated people to pull the best out of themselves to do what was necessary. He was a voice of reason and inspiration when his community needed it.

He established subcommittees for trash removal, mail delivery, recovery loans, public transportation, and utilities, and he regularly met with them for one year. He displayed strong confidence in each of the subcommittee lieutenants to carry out the work they discussed in their meetings, and they did. Under his guidance, the leaders of the Wyoming Valley reconceived and developed a whole new community.

My mentor's message to his community after the flood was one I heard him repeat over the years to local youth. Keep hope alive. Even though your conditions may be limited, there is opportunity. With thought and planning and persistence, you can overcome the obstacles and inadequacies that exist. "In times of great uncertainty and need, you will have doubts," he said. "Also have hopes. Have dreams."

Judge understood that the gravest danger in a crisis is the death of hope. His leadership refocused attention from darkness to light. See the light emanating from within—that is the light of potential. See the light in the distance—that is the light of possibility. See the light directly before you that will illuminate the way as you take a first step, and then another. This is the light of hope.

Among our cherished possessions is Judge's desk from when he first practiced law. He wanted my husband to have it when Monte started out in Pennsylvania in his new profession as a financial advisor. This grand old cherry desk was submerged during the flood and reemerged unscathed. We have taken it with us each time we've moved homes, appreciating its message of resilience.

In one interview, Judge commented, "I don't believe that I've had very much influence in shaping the valley." Thousands of people in the Wyoming Valley touched by his vibrant sense of humanity and compassion for the people of his community would disagree.

The respect shown to him often rose to a level of reverence. People lit up when they heard I was a Rosenn clerk, commenting on how great a man he was. It seemed impossible to walk with him for more than half a block without someone warmly greeting him.

It dawned on me one day that this admiration was unrelated to my mentor's position in the United States judiciary. Few of the locals seemed to care that he was one of the area's most important governmental figures. He was respected as an outstanding leader who served his community with integrity and helped lead in difficult times. Instead of moving to Philadelphia when appointed to the court, he chose to live in his hometown and commute nearly monthly for a week at a time.

Seeing the respect that flowed to Judge not only made me proud to be working as his law clerk, it inspired me. It made me want to be a better person, well beyond my years as a representative of him.

As children, many of us learn the biblical principle *As we sow, so shall we reap.* When we give stingily, we are rewarded meagerly. When we give abundantly, we are rewarded richly. Watching my mentor reap the natural consequence of his intense dedication to his community decades after the flood, I saw this principle in action.

> A noble leader answers not to the trumpet calls of self-promotion but to the hushed whispers of necessity.

In Giving We Receive

"Both Dad and my mother treated the law clerks with extraordinary hospitality. They became part of our extended family, and they have shown their appreciation by generously establishing the Max Rosenn Lecture Series at Wilkes University. This lecture series has brought in outstanding speakers to Wilkes-Barre for the past twenty-six years. It has also been an occasion for the clerks to come back and visit with my father and each other.

"Dad chose his law clerks with great care, and many have gone on to very distinguished careers. They share a fierce loyalty to my father and great pride in having been a Max Rosenn law clerk.

"My father, in turn, was immensely fond of his clerks and loved receiving visits and letters from them. He would attend and even occasionally officiate at their weddings and other family events."

It was a sweltering July day in 1991. From the smoke billowing from under the hood, it appeared that our old Saab was even hotter than we were.

"It's a fine car," the mechanic said as he eyed the car I'd recently bought from a partner at the Michigan law firm where I clerked for the summer. "It just wasn't made to pull that big U-Haul over these mountains."

Despite our snail's pace over the Appalachian Mountains, it was our third stop for overheating. "How many more ranges before Wilkes-Barre?" we asked the mechanic.

"You're almost there. Only one more sizable climb. I can patch you up and you should be able to make it."

We finally arrived and settled into our hotel. Having decided during the drive to hold off on calling Judge until we'd found an apartment, we set out with newspaper classifieds in hand.

If you've ever apartment hunted on a newlywed's budget, you know the frustrations: too run down, too expensive, uninhabitable. Given the sprawl of the Wyoming Valley and our unfamiliarity with any of the dozens of boroughs, we zigzagged our way east and west, north and south, crossing off listing after listing.

At the end of our second full day of apartment hunting—and the night before the U-Haul was due back—we reviewed our options. We settled on a condo in Nanticoke, a borough that had seen its heyday during the flourishing coal industry in the 1930s.

When the mining evaporated, so had its prosperity, leaving behind boarded up stores and long lines at the unemployment office. Living there would require a thirty-minute commute to work each way in the single car we shared, but it was the best of our options as we knew them.

We had toured the condo the day before. The landlords, George and Gerry, were a pleasant retired couple. They lived in the adjoining condo, which gave us a sense of safety. The rent was on the high end of our budget, but after all of the small and dirty places we'd seen, it looked like a good deal to us.

We arrived in Nanticoke early evening, prepared to tell our new landlords of our decision. They weren't home so we grabbed a bite to eat. We stopped by after dinner, and they still weren't home. After waiting another couple hours at a public park down the street, we were beginning to worry. What if they'd gone away for the night? Finally, at 10:30, we saw car lights.

We met them as they were getting out of their car. "Hi! Remember us? We've decided we'd like to rent your condo."

Showing surprise, George said, "We're just back from a day at the Jersey shore and are ready to settle in for the night."

"This won't take long." I assured him. "Our U-Haul is just down the street, and we're ready to move in."

"The condo isn't wired for electricity," he said, shaking his head. "We'll try to have it ready to go by mid-next week."

"Umm. We were planning to empty the U-Haul tonight," Monte replied gingerly. "We need to return it by six tomorrow morning or have to pay extra." In our minds, we already were their new tenants. I guess they needed a little time to catch up to our decision.

We almost lost George. He then caught his wife's eye. His face slowly softened into a mixed look of resignation and compassion. He apparently was able to see us for the naive, young couple we were, a pair of green kids who hadn't yet learned that simply because *you* make a decision doesn't mean it's made in another person's mind.

"I'll go get some extension cords and see what I can do to rig up some lighting in your new home," he said gruffly. He walked off, slapping his hands together as he got to work. Gerry smiled at us.

Recalling the youthful drama of that night has brought many laughs over the years. Yet, the funniest part was our assumption that Judge wouldn't want to hear from us until we were all settled in our new home.

By the time we called, he expressed concern about not having heard from us and disappointedly told us that he had lined up several apartments for our viewing in more respectable and convenient locations. Although he preferred us to live closer to his home, he didn't suggest we break our lease. He would later travel to Nanticoke with housewarming gifts, searching among our cardboard-box furniture draped with secondhand tablecloths for things to compliment.

We had not yet heard story after story of how Judge assisted, not only finding housing but also arranging car loans, cosigning loans at the bank, arranging special deals, and even lending apartment furnishings until clerks could provide their own.

We did not yet know that Judge immediately took the spouses of his law clerks under his wing, ensuring that they found suitable employment during their year in Wilkes-Barre, and he rolled out the red carpet for any family that came to visit during the year.

We did not yet know that we'd be welcomed not only by Judge but also by his family and friends, enjoying frequent dinners, holiday celebrations, nights at the symphony, and weekends at his summer cottage.

We did not yet know that we would learn from a master how to balance the demands of being professionals, intensely dedicated to our work, while equally committed to our family, friends, and community.

We did not yet know that clerking for Judge meant not only acquiring a boss but also a mentor, teacher, father figure, career advisor, marriage counselor, and lifelong friend. We could not foresee the extraordinary integrity, kindness, generosity, and depth of character we were going to experience over the coming years by his side.

Can you feel the magic that transpired within a Rosenn clerkship? It is the magic that flows from an open heart. A vessel open to receiving all of the abundance that God has to offer and to overflow with its goodness. As this abundance is poured out to uplift others, the vessel expands to love more deeply and share more fully.

An open heart carries within the perspective of selflessness— a lesson my husband and I sorely needed schooling in as a young couple.

> The more you become aware of and respond to the needs of others, the richer your own life becomes.

There Was a Teacher

"Dad somehow always managed to have time for family and for friends, which was very important to him. Some of my fondest memories are of the times we played golf together.

"I was very fortunate to have had him as a role model.

"Dad took great pride in the accomplishments of his children, grandchildren, and great-grandchildren. He was extremely generous to all of us during his lifetime, not only financially but, more importantly, with love and support.

Struggling to keep his composure, Keith concluded, "We shall miss him dearly."

As the story goes, a young Johns Hopkins professor assigned his graduate students to go to the slums to study high-risk juveniles. They connected with two hundred boys between the ages of twelve and sixteen, investigating their background and environment. The students talked to the boys, compiled the data, and ran the numbers to predict the boys' chances for the future. Given the risk factors, they predicted that 90 percent of the boys would spend some time in jail.

Twenty-five years later another group of graduate students was given the job of testing the prediction. They returned to the area, talked to the men who were still there, tracked down ones who had moved, and recorded the few who had died. They managed to get in touch with a hundred and eighty of the original two hundred. They found that only four of the group had ever been sent to jail.

Why was it that these men, who had lived in a breeding place of crime, had such a surprisingly good record? The researchers were continually told: "Well, there was a teacher . . ."

Upon further investigation, the researchers found that 75 percent of the men referred to the same teacher. The researchers went to this woman's home in search of answers. How had she exerted this remarkable influence over that group of children? Could she give them any reason why these boys should have remembered her?

"No," the retired teacher answered. "No, I really couldn't." And then she got a faraway look in her eyes, and the researchers could see her travel back in time over the years. Murmuring more to herself than to her interviewers she recalled, "I loved those boys..."

Judge was not demonstrative with "I love you's." He ended our phone calls with a safer version: "I send my love" or "Take care, my dear, and please give my love to Monte and the children." It was by his deeds, not his words, that his love could be seen and felt. He demonstrated it through caring about and remembering the small details of others' lives.

Long after Judge passed, conversation with him still came easily with his photos on my desk. My kids joked about those wise eyes that seemed to follow us around and the smile that turned up just a bit when we were feeling our greatest joy.

When writing this book, I took a trip back to Philadelphia, the city where we attended sittings of the court. As I was walking across the park toward the Liberty Bell, a path we had often walked together, I felt him. It was as if my friend and mentor physically was walking across Liberty Park, step-by-step, alongside me.

A wave of gratitude washed over me as I felt Judge's presence with such clarity and strength. I continued to walk the streets of Philadelphia where we had shared many walks and talks, immersed in warmth.

Reflecting on how Judge would respond if he'd been alive and we'd discussed this experience, I recalled a story he told about his mother. Jennie had befriended a beautiful woman from Paris who'd married an American soldier, only to find herself living in the basement of his parents' home in rural Pennsylvania. One day, Jennie had a strong feeling that her friend was not okay. She followed her intuition and swiftly drove her buggy down to the river's edge, arriving just in time to see her friend jump from the bridge. She leaped into the water and saved the bride's life. She later advised the well-intentioned soldier, "Your wife can never be happy here. She needs the museums, music, and culture of the city. I will nurse her back to health while you go to New York. Send for her when you find a job and an apartment." He did as suggested, and the couple happily lived out their years raising their family in the city.

Judge viewed his mother's ability to "know" what was going to happen as a natural result of her profound level of wisdom, common sense, and understanding of human nature. He'd likely find a similarly rational explanation for how I was able to once again enjoy his company on a beautiful Saturday evening in Philadelphia.

I later connected the peace I felt in those moments with Judge to another experience in my life. It was 1998, and I'd been up throughout the night, desperately ill from food poisoning. Monte had gotten out of bed to check on me. I heard his voice from outside of the bathroom as I was folded over in pain. "Mollie, are you okay?"

"I'm dying, I'm dying," I moaned. "I'm dying." I tried to walk toward him and collapsed on the floor.

Moments later, I could see Monte in the kitchen, two rooms away, calling 9-1-1. *I could see him.*

Looking down, I could see me. How fascinating.

With great curiosity, I watched my husband rushing around in a frenzy. He was clumsily putting a pair of his black running shorts on me, apparently in an attempt to make me more presentable for the emergency personnel. How thoughtful he was, even in an emergency.

I was by the side of my nearly four-year-old son, Nate. I kissed him good-bye. "Your dad will take good care of you." It was not really a thought, more just a knowing.

In the next instant, I was leaning over my daughter's crib. Such a beautiful baby you are. Feeling pure love, I gently kissed her good-bye. We would meet again when the time was to be.

I was floating higher, ready to move through the ceiling. No pain. No attachment. Simply peace.

"Mollie, don't leave me. Stay with me, Mollie. Stay with me. *Don't leave me.*"

The angst in my husband's voice momentarily stopped me. I looked down at him leaning over my body. His hands on each of my arms, shaking me. Begging and pleading.

I saw them just before I felt it. The medical team rushed through our front door toward me.

Whoosh.

I was back in my body. On a stretcher, being carefully slid into an ambulance.

Perhaps it was this near death experience that helped me stay open when Judge appeared by my side in Philadelphia. Whatever allowed it, the memory of this experience has taken residence in a piece of my heart where I hope it lives forever.

Logical, legalistic minds may dismiss this as metaphysical hogwash. I agree that it defies logic. But logic cannot fully explain matters of the heart. The story of Judge as a mentor is a love story. And love unites people not just for this lifetime but beyond.

> Your greatest path of influence is love.

In Service to Destiny

When Keith finished his eulogy, Rabbi Larry Kaplan stood to speak. "The Scriptures say a man should live seventy years, and Max Rosenn knew this passage well. These stories from his life reveal a man who did not fear passing.

"Not long ago the Judge said, 'When the good Lord issues His last summons for me, I'm prepared to go without any recrimination. Life has been good to me, it owes me nothing.'"

Rabbi Rosenberg then observed: "Judge's faith had a great impact on his life. He attended temple every week and prayed often. Unlike those who believe they must sacrifice their faith for their profession, Max Rosenn's Jewish faith never waned despite a career in a secular field.

"He was a man who never appeared disheveled or without a tie.

Yet, he wouldn't let his son shave him in the hospital just a few weeks ago. He had just come off the respirator that Saturday morning after three brutal, painful days. He was groggy but oriented. When his son asked if he could shave him, Max whispered, 'Wait until the Sabbath is over.'"

My mentor used to quote his mother as saying, "These old bones don't owe me anything." She taught him that we must work diligently each day. We must earn our rewards. We shape our lives and ourselves by being responsible for our choices. He fully assumed responsibility for his thoughts, words, actions, and the results he produced in his life.

My mentor's view of destiny reflected an intimate integration between his religious beliefs and his free will. While he embraced a strong sense of personal destiny, he did not see life as completely controlled by a higher power because of man's ability to alter his life by what he does and the choices he makes.

He believed that all who seek a meaningful life must test their talents and put them to their greatest use. He chose to use his talents to foster respect, promote justice, and preserve liberty. He guided me to say yes to requests to serve when I had a worthy contribution to make, and leave the rest of the details to God.

Although we practiced different religions, the role religion played in his life resonated with me. Judge explained, "My religion instilled in me qualities of faith, courage, hope, a sense of responsibility, and a belief that life was divinely controlled. I came to believe that we are not captains of our own destiny but that there is a higher order. Not only in our life but also in the stars and heavens, the formation of animals and the birds, and all the organisms that comprise life. There is something else besides ourselves that determines the causes of life, destiny, and the future."

Yet, his religion and belief in some divine control over life did not eradicate his belief in the power of choice. He embraced this paradox, "If we didn't feel that an individual can shape one's life, we wouldn't be concerned with developments of character and fundamental precepts like justice, the value of truth, the redeeming power of compassion, and the transforming power of love. There are events that came into my life as a youth. These events can spur you on and elevate your goals or have the opposite effect. My sense is that they spurred me on."

My mentor taught me that destiny whispers softly. It does

not shout. It is not a bully, pushing us where we don't want to go. It quietly nods to the choices we make. Over time, the consequences of these choices shape our destiny.

Judge experienced great challenges in his long life that easily could have destroyed him as they did countless others. He lived through the Great Depression, several wars, discrimination, a historic flood, and the injury and death of loved ones. He experienced many of the more insidious destroyers of men, like power, prestige, and wealth. It took great strength of character to hold on to the core of who he was. He did so with grace.

His success was built on his choice to see each event life brought to him as an opportunity to respond with action that elevated himself and all around him. He chose to live righteously. He chose honesty in his business affairs. He chose to invest himself in his relationships. He chose to set aside time daily to renew and strengthen himself. He chose to relentlessly work toward a more just world. He chose to amass riches that would outlast his days on earth.

His life stands as a reminder that we continue shaping our legacy until our final day. It is the choices we make each day in the little things, when no one is watching, that set our course. We can choose good or evil, love or hatred, generosity or selfishness. The choices of our lives are recorded in the memories of others.

In our family, friends, acquaintances, and, especially, those we help and those we turn away from.

Our choices have consequences, good or bad, that accrue to mark our life as a success or failure long after we're gone. They marked the life of Max Rosenn a success.

> Our power lies in our small
> daily choices, one after another,
> to create eternal ripples of
> a life well lived.

The Finale

The flag was draped over the coffin. The pallbearers rolled the casket down the aisle. The crowd followed in silent respect. The doors to the synagogue opened.

We sat in our car, watching as Judge's community of mourners streamed into the bright February morning.

A line of cars began making its way to the cemetery. Monte looked at me. No words were needed. None would be sufficient. We joined the procession.

Epilogue: Wherever I Go

I came to his service as a young lawyer, convinced that greatness was ahead of me and I would have to run hard to find it. At a deep level, I knew I was designed for something bigger. I thought the way to catch it was to run fast or forever lose out on the opportunity.

Spending time by my mentor's side in the stillness of his chambers, this perspective seemed absurd. What exactly was I rushing for? To chase a big career? To make millions? To find my destiny?

His life revealed the power of slowing down in a way that allowed me to see the opportunities before me and cocreate my destiny. *Be still, and let your path reveal itself.*

I cannot tell you that I stayed fully connected to this

understanding of life upon leaving my mentor's side. The road was not so smooth.

My clerkship was no less profound than a heart transplant. My heart ticked differently after my time with Judge. Yet, it took years of experience and perspective for my body to fully accept and function with my new heart.

I followed my clerkship with graduate schooling as a social scientist. Daily bathing in scientific research and academia nurtured my analytical and logical nature. The competitor within me rose to the challenge, graduating first in my class in graduate school as I had with my undergraduate degree.

I studied by the side of new teachers. More than one taught their most profound lessons through missteps.

An even greater challenge came a couple years after Judge's death. My life then looked very different from the harmonious balance that he brought to his days. I'd scored a book contract with a New York publishing house and was working long hours to complete the manuscript while running full steam ahead with my consulting work and raising my family.

One evening I felt stabbing pains in my chest and thought that maybe I had pulled a muscle. The next day, in the middle of a session with a client, my thinking suddenly became fuzzy, as though my brain had been wrapped in wool. I headed home, but as I began driving, I felt so off-kilter that I drove straight to a doctor's office instead.

Initial tests indicated a heart attack or pulmonary embolism—surprising conditions for a woman in her early forties. The doctor sent me directly to the hospital for additional tests. The following weeks were a blur of medical appointments, bed rest, and trips to the emergency room when symptoms took a sharp turn for the worse.

Finally, my internist determined that a virus had gone into my heart, wreaking havoc on my ability to function. Doctor after doctor failed to provide any solutions that improved my condition. The pathogens flourished, eventually spreading to my nervous system.

My body went completely haywire. At times, I lost my ability to walk and I couldn't talk clearly. On a few terrifying mornings, I woke up in a cloud of gray, unable to see the world around me.

I was confined to bed for weeks. Slowly, I began to build up the amount of time that I could get out of bed to be with my family or simply to take a shower. Yet I was weak and exhausted and nowhere near able to work or even drive a car.

One day, when my husband was off entertaining the kids, I got out of bed to make a cup of tea. My laptop was sitting in the corner, long untouched. I was drawn to it. I opened my email and an announcement of a business seminar by a consultant from Pennsylvania appeared in my inbox.

It was as if the invitation had hands that reached out, grabbed my shirt, and pulled me right into the computer. I was certain that something about the seminar was going to help me heal. With the cautious support of my husband, I flew across the country. The seminar was solid, but I didn't see how it was going to alleviate my illness. Disappointed, I wondered why I'd been so strongly drawn to come.

The last evening, I was so weak that I changed my plans to go into New York City with some participants. I decided to join a few others for a quick dinner in the hotel before heading to bed. I sat next to a man named Karl. We exchanged the usual "What do you do?" questions.

He was a holistic health practitioner; I tried not to let my skepticism show. Still, I found myself telling him about my illness and the cardiac virus that had attacked my body. In response, Karl told me a story of a driver in a horse-pulled cart, with a silent passenger sitting in the back.

"Your horse," Karl began, "oh, your horse is a beauty. A thoroughbred stallion. If it were a car, it would be a Ferrari . . . a six-cylinder Ferrari. But it has been forced to run and run without proper care. It is tired. Dangerously tired.

"And your driver. Your driver is one of the strongest-willed drivers I've seen. An ironclad will.

"Now, your cart needs some attention. With the driver pushing your horse to run so hard, the cart has lost a wheel." He paused then added softly, "It needs mending."

Allowing me some moments for my mind to catch up to what he was saying, Karl asked, "Do you know what your horse represents?"

"My heart?"

"Yes, your heart," he replied, nodding. He repeated softly, "A beautiful stallion. And how about your driver?"

"My mind?"

"Yes, your ego. Yours is strong. You've pushed through many things in your life, haven't you?"

I simply nodded, not wanting to interrupt the unfolding scenario by acknowledging the challenges I'd faced and the family members and loved ones I'd lost over the years.

"And how about your cart?"

"My body." I found myself quietly mirroring Karl's observation, "And it desperately needs mending."

It was Karl's turn to nod. He sat without saying a word.

"How about the silent passenger in the back?" I finally asked.

"Yes," he said. "How about the silent passenger in the back?"

His questioning and gentle way of interacting reminded me of Judge. With a nod, I acknowledged his invitation to explore the status of my relationship with my spirit.

As we talked, Karl suggested a powerful life affirmation: "Wherever I go, wherever I am, I am in love."

In love with what? I thought. "What do you mean by that?" I asked. I defaulted to the linear part of my brain to try to provide an answer. "You mean wherever you go, you show love to others? Or do you mean wherever you go, you love God?"

Still thinking I needed to know all the answers, I exclaimed, "Oh! I know what you mean. You mean you always love yourself, right?"

Karl smiled at me and said in the gentlest of tones, "Mollie, love . . . is *love* . . . isn't it?"

I stared at him for a moment, considering his simplistic statement. Then, suddenly, I felt a great shift within me. *Love* is *love*. It doesn't matter for what. You can *live in love* no matter who you are or where you go. Love is a state of *being*.

Hearing Karl's simple words somehow dropped walls that I'd built around my heart. In a flash, I could see that the love I had for my husband and my kids, in its essence, wasn't different than the love I had for my friends or my clients or my work. It was no different than the love I felt for my God or was called to share with strangers and all of humanity.

Love was an energy flowing through me. It was the energy I watched flow through Judge every day I was with him.

That moment marked the beginning of my permanent transition out of living dominantly in my head. Something inside had opened. It felt as though love was everywhere, as if I'd come around a bend in the road and suddenly a breathtaking view of the ocean appeared, a huge expanse of blue stretching to the horizon and taking me with it.

Love felt bigger and more available than I ever thought it could be. I hadn't learned anything like this in my twenty-five years of formal education.

Karl and I talked through the night. Tears streamed down my face as ideas he shared soaked into my newly opened mind—and heart.

Upon returning home, I used techniques he showed me to monitor my erratic heartbeat, heal my weakened heart, and ease my fatigue and weakness. In the following weeks, I watched in wonder and gratitude as my health swiftly returned.

Today I'm healthy and powerfully reconnected to my life's work of helping others become the best version of themselves.

I've expanded my speaking and mentoring to help leaders thrive, serve more people and their communities, and make a bigger impact in this world. I'm growing my mission to empower children to own the unique goodness they carry within and to give and receive the love that creates healthy adults.

Best of all, love—that pure, flowing energy of the heart—has become the basis of living and decision making in my business as well as my personal life. This has filled me with a consistent joy that I touched upon as a young lawyer by Judge's side.

Sometimes words are just words. You hear them and they seem trite or superficial or cliché. Other times they open a door deep within, and your world is turned inside out.

"Wherever I go, wherever I am, I am in love" was a seed. Falling on the fertile ground prepared by my life's greatest mentor, it took hold.

This simple but profound truth shifted my left-brain expertise to its proper place, nested on the power of my heart. My body fully accepted my new heart. My transplant was complete.

I was now able to return to all of the lessons taught by Judge and see them in the wholeness in which they were offered. With this broader perspective, I could see anew this truth taught by a wise judge to a young lawyer—that even in the logical, analytical world of law, it is the heart that is central to delivering justice.

Acknowledgments

It took a community to bring Judge's story to life. He wouldn't have wanted it any other way.

Harold, Sallyanne, Keith, Sylvia, Daniel, Barbara, Eva, and the extended Rosenn family, your support of this book as a labor of love means the world to me. Thank you for helping me bring your beloved patriarch to life for others. And to the loving memory of Tillie, Lillian, and Florence, classy and sassy women way ahead of their time. The love and enduring pride your family members have for each other sets the bar high. Being a member of your *mishpocha* has gifted me memories of a lifetime.

Joe Savitz, your brilliance comes through in this story, and you are even more shining in life. In a movie of Judge's life, Hollywood could not cast a more perfect man to play the role of his first law clerk. It was part of your destiny to step into this role, and you fulfilled it beautifully.

Virginia Transue, sharing love and admiration for the man you dutifully served has made this journey ever more special. You always had his back. Whenever I was at a loss for words to describe the vastness of his life, I was tempted to fall back on that little descriptor you say in your northeast Pennsylvanian accent to sum him up perfectly: "What a guy."

Rosenn law clerks, I list you by name in this book with the greatest love and respect. You continue to do Judge proud. Rick Matasar, thank you for introducing me to this great man and to the greatness of this man. Tina Sciocchetti, Avi Szenberg, and Tom Brown—memories of our year together in Wilkes-Barre still warm my heart. And a special thank-you for your unconditional support upon the unveiling of this book: Paul MacGregor, Hal Kwalwasser, Linda Fisher, Diana Donaldson, Norm Monhait, Fred Magaziner, Jim Sandman, Ron Krauss, Craig Blakely, Richard Gelfond, Jeff Goldsmith, Harrison Cohen, Steve Cohen, Jennie Sikes, Jonah Zimiles, Andy Morris, Susan Gellman, Diane Klotnia, Heather McRay, Quentin Palfrey, and Joe Cosgrove.

Bob Burg, our cherished friendship, your gracious foreword, and the joy it has brought me to see you adopt my beloved mentor as your own are invaluable treasures.

Thank you to my friends, teachers, and cheerleaders for seeing the promise of this story, many of you before a word was set to paper: Gus and Fran Columbus, Tom Peters, Mark Oakes, Mark Silver, Michael Port, Debbie Bermont, Dan Pink, Marci Shimoff, Frank McKinney, Marsh Ulrich, Larina Kase, and Fran Ponick. Your support made this book a better read and me a better person. And to all who found your way to the pages of this story, including dear ones Kelley and Karl.

I bow my head in gratitude to Aaron Foster, Linda Charbonneau, Ericka Van Hook, Minesh Patel, Sue Nail, and Dylan Jordan for your dedication to helping me share Judge's message and life to help others. I also greatly appreciate the support of my twelve siblings and their families and my in-laws, who removed the "in-law" from our relationship and have always made me feel like another daughter and sister.

Thanks to my all-star Greenleaf team. Chris McRay, every author needs a good quarterback and you ran the production of this book like a pro. Jay Hodges, I'm grateful not only for your talented editing but also for your holding a vision for the impact of this book. Sheila Parr, you captured my mentor's essence with your design: simple elegance.

Dr. Richard Abramowitz and your nurse, Bonnie Hasiak, you moved mountains (and more than a little protocol) to arrange

Judge's treatments and care during his final years to allow him to continue doing his great work in the world. You gave to my mentor time, attention, and love far beyond your medical duties. Thank you.

Ann Smith, my dear friend who spent weeks of Wednesdays with Judge during my clerkship interviewing our noble mentor. Your work at Life Stories Remembered strengthened this book and helped me honor him.

Tony Mussari and lovely Kitch. Watching you be inspired by greatness and taking courageous action to share the fruits of your inspiration with others has been life changing.

This book, and in many ways my life, begins and ends with you, Monte. You are the one who said, "You *must* go learn from this man," not knowing that we'd be married by the time my clerkship began. You sacrificed greatly to start our life together in Pennsylvania and have continued to support me in countless ways over the past twenty years. This is why I laughed when my co-clerk asked, "Does it bother you that Judge likes Monte better than he likes either of us?" What are the chances of having a life mentor and a husband cut from the same cloth? I'm grateful for this every single day.

To Nate, born a wise soul like my mentor. You told me that my first drafts weren't the best I could do, and you were right. To Alaina, who played the starring role in one of my favorite memories with Judge. Sometimes the best material ends up on the cutting room floor. I promise your "Goodbye, Max!" story will come to life at www.walkingwithjustice.com. And Erin, you sat and wrote your first book as I wrote mine. You're the best writing partner a mom could ever hope for.

Finally, to Judge. I would dedicate this book to your memory, but you continue to remain vibrantly alive to me. Whenever I struggled with my mission to bring your goodness and wisdom to others, I felt your gentle guidance, "You sit, I'll write." I made a promise to you at your funeral, which I celebrate fulfilling with this book. It has been the greatest honor of my life to share your story. I hereby make another promise: *"Judge, I will be relentless in living up to all you taught me as I continue to bring your love and lessons to the world."*

Rosenn Law Clerks

Name	Year of Service	Name	Year of Service
Bill Robertson	1970–71	Mary Ann Bobinski	1987–88
Wm. Paul MacGregor	1970–71	Joseph Zwicker	1987–88
Harold Kwalwasser	1971–72	Diane Klotnia	1988–89
John Osborn Jr.	1971–72	Tracy Smith	1988–89
Timothy Hardy	1972–73	James Harshaw	1989–90
Clarence Kegel Jr.	1972–73	Michael Rosenthal	1989–90
Linda Fisher	1973–74	Timothy Cahn	1990–91
Michael Scher	1973–74	Heather McRay	1990–91
Mike Selter	1974–75	Tina Sciocchetti	1991–92
David Thomas	1974–75	Mollie Marti	1991–92, 1993–95
Diana Donaldson	1975–76	Deborah Koconis	1992–93
Norman Monhait	1975–76	Daniel Young	1992–93
Fred Magaziner	1976–77	Avi Szenberg	1993–94
James Sandman	1976–77	Thomas Brown	1994–95
Ronald Krauss	1977–78	Karen Coombs	1995–96
Richard Matasar	1977–78	Pamela Hunt	1995–96
Daniel Koffsky	1978–79	Kathleen Laubenstein	1996–97
Richard Schifter	1978–79	Rose Weber	1996–97
Craig Blakeley	1979–80	Richard Zack	1997–98
Richard Gelfond	1979–80	David Dargatis	1997–98
Jeffrey Goldsmith	1979–80	Craig Buckser	1998–99
Harrison Cohen	1980–81	JT Stephen Crane	1998–99
Ford Huffman	1980–81	Larry Reich	1999–2000
Joseph Seiler III	1980–81	Shaun Simmons	1999–2000
Steven Cohen	1981–82	Jonathan Pressman	2000–2001
Virginia Sikes	1981–82	ToniAnn Grande	2000–2001
V. Elizabeth Grayson	1982–83	Gaurav Shah	2001–2
Jeffrey Lowenthal	1982–83	David Wolf	2001–2
Peter Rofes	1983–84	Paul Edenfield	2002–3
Jonah Zimiles	1983–84	Quentin Palfrey	2002–3
Miriam Clark	1984–85	Ray Chan	2003–4
Steven Weingarten	1984–85	Stephen Albrecht	2003–4
Andrew Morris	1985–86	Michelle Kenney	2004–5
Richard Zarin	1985–86	Brian Wildstein	2004–5
Brad Friedman	1986–87	Anne Champion	2005–6
Susan Gellman	1986–87	Coulter Paulsen	2005–6

Ode to a Mentor

Speech given by law clerk James J. Sandman
Dedication of Portrait of Judge Max Rosenn
Federal Courthouse, Philadelphia
June 14, 2002

May it please the Court.

Most people who view the portrait unveiled here today will never know the man it depicts. They may well know of him through the 873 published opinions he has authored thus far, and through the considerable reputation he has developed in his thirty-two years as a member of this court and in his seventy years as a member of the bar. For those who do not and never will know Judge Rosenn personally, I would like to try to provide, for the record of this proceeding, a description of the character of the man in the picture.

Judge Rosenn's clerks know him well. And he knows us well. The strength of our relationships is in part a function of the location of the Judge's chambers in Wilkes-Barre. Almost all of Judge Rosenn's clerks are not from northeastern Pennsylvania; almost all of us spent a year of our lives in Wilkes-Barre solely because we wanted to work for and be with Judge Rosenn. The Judge has always felt himself responsible for many—make that most—aspects of his clerks' lives during their year in Wilkes-Barre. For example, no reunion of Rosenn clerks is complete without a raucous recounting of the Judge's many efforts to find mates, or at least dates, for those who entered his service unattached.

The Judge takes his clerks into his family. We know his brother Harold and his sister Lillian and we knew his late sister Florence, who delighted in confiding to us that the Judge, whose penchant for formality is readily apparent, wears a rubber necktie when he takes a shower.

We know his sons, Keith and Daniel. And those of us who clerked for Judge Rosenn in his first twenty-two years on the bench also knew, and loved, his remarkable wife Tillie, who was our friend, our counselor, and our coconspirator.

But the strength of his clerks' relationships with Judge Rosenn is a function of far more than our having spent time together in a place that was new for us. It is a function of the person that he is—of his kindness, his thoughtfulness, his generosity, his genuine concern for others. These qualities pervade not only his personal relationships, they pervade the way he approaches his judicial responsibilities. Notwithstanding the isolation of his professional life on an appellate court, Judge Rosenn never loses sight of the human consequences of the work he does. I recall the Judge reminding me repeatedly during the year I clerked for him that each case before the Court involved real people, who understandably regarded their case as the most important on the docket. The care and attention he devotes to each case reflect that sensitivity.

I have thought many times over the twenty-six years I have known him about how much I have learned, and continue to learn, from Judge Rosenn. At the top of a very long list, two things stand out in my mind. The first is the importance of treating everyone with whom you deal—everyone—with respect.

It was this quality—showing respect as a matter of recognizing the dignity of every person—that I noticed first when I met Judge Rosenn on that day he interviewed me for a clerkship. He took me out to lunch in Wilkes-Barre that day. I thought that was just extraordinary—a Circuit Judge taking a law student out to lunch. As we walked to our dining place, I was struck by the fact that the Judge knew and spoke to every single person we passed. What struck me even more, though, was how the people we passed spoke to him, and how he spoke to them. Their admiration and respect for him was palpable. And so, too, was his respect for them. For every person, whatever his or her station in life, the Judge stopped and gave of his time and attention and made him or her feel important.

I saw that quality—treating others with respect as a fundamental part of all his dealings with others—repeatedly during my clerkship. I saw it in the way Judge Rosenn spoke of his fellow judges on this Court, explaining to my co-clerk, Fred Magaziner, and me what special qualities and experience and perspectives each brought to the judicial process.

I saw it in the way he wrote opinions. He would not permit himself to use the term "lower court" to describe a District Court, because he regarded that term as disrespectful of a fellow judge. I saw it in the way he treated the lawyers who appeared before him—even, perhaps especially, those who were not as prepared as they should have been. I saw it in the way he treated court employees. And I felt it in the way he treated me, a nervous and inexperienced twenty-five-year-old. He treated me as a valued professional colleague, and he made me feel like a million bucks.

The second item on my "top two" list of lessons from Judge Rosenn is the importance of community service. I cannot recall a day when the Judge did not spend some time—at lunch or in the evening—on one or more of his many community projects. Doing good for others is a part of every day of his life. He did not talk much about this; he taught the lesson by example. The power of his conduct said it all: of those to whom much is given, much is expected.

It is a great blessing to start out in one's career at the elbow of a role model—a person who inspires you, who motivates you to be better than you are, a person you want to be like. That is how we Rosenn clerks started our careers as lawyers. And the inspiration never fades. This man, whose life proves that human kindness and professional success need never be inconsistent, and can in fact promote each other, still sets the standard for those of us who clerked for him many years ago.

What I am trying to say is that the man in the picture is a hero.

One of the benefits of a long life lived well and in good health is that those who love you do not want for opportunities to tell you so. I speak for all of your clerks, Judge, in saying that we love you. We thank you for all you have done and continue to do for us. And each of us blesses the day that the path of your life crossed the path of ours.

Thank you.

Bonus Chapters

The lessons of Judge Max Rosenn go far beyond what you hold in your hands. There was much more material I wanted to include in this book that I couldn't due to space constraints.

These lessons and stories are gifts that I promised Judge I would share. I do this through my website and speaking. Visit me at www.walkingwithjustice.com to find out more.

Here are just a few examples of the exclusive reader-only content you will find at this special website dedicated to bringing you more of Judge's wisdom:

- Videos and photos
- Bonus chapters
- Interviews
- Mentorship tools

In these pages, you experienced Judge as a steward of all he'd been given. In his honor, one-tenth of the profits on every book will be donated to philanthropy. Beneficiaries include the Community Resiliency Project, an organization that supports communities through crisis recovery and resiliency education.

It is my heartfelt wish that you will use this book and reader support to step into the life of an extraordinary teacher and allow his guidance to lift you up and remind you of the greatness you have within.

You've taken the first step by reading this book. Ready to put more of Judge's wisdom into action in your life? I will do everything I can to support you.

Visit me today at www.walkingwithjustice.com for more uncommon lessons from one of life's greatest mentors.

About the Author

Mollie Marti is a psychologist, lawyer, and adjunct professor at the University of Iowa Department of Psychology. She speaks around the globe, training corporations, universities, and associations on leadership resilience, servant mentorship, life design, and business ethics.

Dr. Mollie brings years of experience in coaching a prestigious list of clients, including Olympians and business elites, to her work as founding editor of the *Best Life Design* e-magazine. She also hosts the popular Make an Impact Live event, raising philanthropic funds while empowering leaders and business professionals to thrive financially in a way that fuels their health, relationships, and greatest life priorities.

Mollie graduated first in her class in both undergraduate and graduate school and from the Iowa College of Law with high distinction. In addition to authoring several law and academic journal articles, her two business success books have been published in several languages.

Grateful to receive a second chance after her life deconstructed from a cardiac virus and inspired by her mentor's example, Dr. Mollie extended her peak performance work to mentorship programs for low opportunity youth and communities in crisis. She currently is founder of the non-profit Community Resiliency Project and actively partners with other charitable organizations.

With her unique ability to combine the science of success with the art of exceptional living, Dr. Mollie is a frequent resource for local and national media. She lives on an apple orchard in scenic northeast Iowa with her husband, Monte, their three beautiful children, Nate, Alaina, and Erin, and large family of pets.

To contact Mollie or find out where to hear her speak, visit www.DrMollie.com.